ENGLISH HERITA
IN STAINED GLASS:
OXFORD

Michael Archer, Sarah Crewe and Peter Cormack

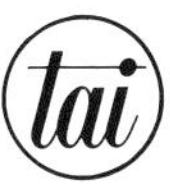

Oxford, England and New York, USA

Published by Trans Atlantic Investments Limited
Blair House, 3 Church Lane, Somerton, Oxon. OX5 4NB, UK
92 Ferris Lane, Poughkeepsie, New York, NY 12603, USA

The first volume in the ENGLISH HERITAGE IN STAINED GLASS series, editor Sarah Crewe.

Designed by Wendy Meagher
Typeset in Baskerville
Colour separations and studio work by Oxford Litho Plates Ltd., Oxford
Printed in Great Britain by KNP Group Ltd., Redditch

British Library Cataloguing in Publication Data
Archer, Michael
English heritage in stained glass: Oxford.—
(English heritage in stained glass).
1. England. Churches. Stained windows.
Glass, to 1987
I. Title II. Crewe, Sarah III. Cormack, Peter
748.592

ISBN 1 871144 01 9 ISBN 1 871144 02 7 Pbk

Library of Congress Cataloging in Publication Data

Archer, Michael.
English heritage in stained glass.

Bibliography: p.
Includes index.
1. Glass painting and staining—English—Oxford (Oxfordshire)—History. I. Crewe, Sarah. II. Cormack, Peter. III. Title.
NK5344.08A74 1988 748.592′574 88 12284

ISBN 1 871144 01 9 ISBN 1 871144 02 7 (pbk.)

CONTENTS

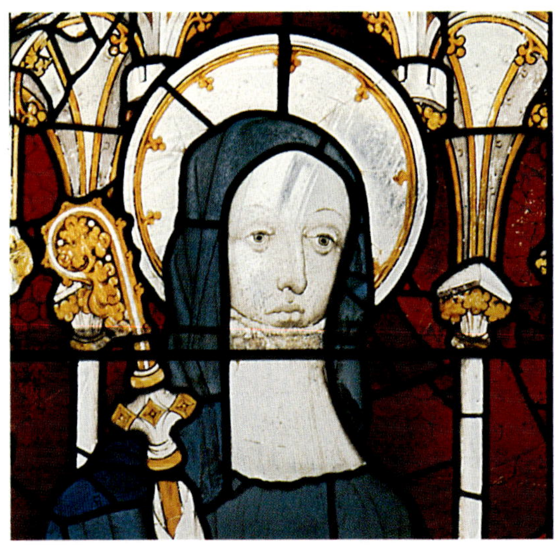
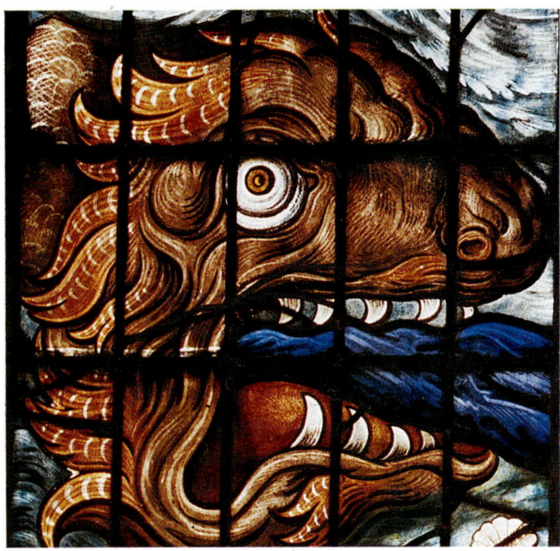
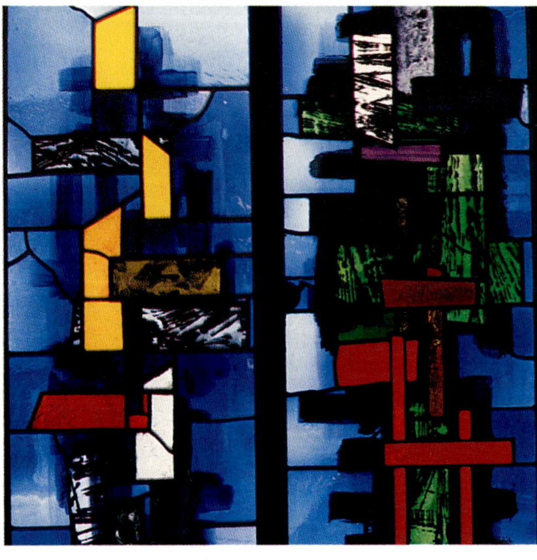

INTRODUCTION

The city of Oxford contains one of the finest collections of stained glass anywhere in the world. Almost every style and period of English glass-painting is represented, from the Gothic age to modern times, often in examples of remarkable quality and importance. From the 13th-century medieval glass of Merton College chapel to John Piper's windows at Nuffield, and from the New College chapel glass of the late 14th century to the flowering of the Gothic Revival in the Victorian period, all are preserved in Oxford.

It was the establishment of a university in Oxford during the 13th century that was to ensure its future as a great city. The reputation of glass-painters strengthened in the late 14th century under William of Wykeham, Bishop of Winchester, Chancellor of England, when he chose an Oxford workshop to glaze his colleges in Oxford and Winchester. The English Reformation of the early 16th century had a disastrous effect on the traditional ecclesiastical arts, not least the art of stained glass. The 17th century, however, was to be one of renewed building activity with architects such as Sir Christopher Wren and Nicholas Hawksmoor, and under James I and Charles I glass-painters found themselves once more in demand.

In the 19th century, the Oxford Movement sought to reintroduce the Catholic pre-Reformation tradition into the English church by way of reintroducing the Gothic style, the style of medieval Christendom. The windows of Pugin, Holiday, Burne-Jones and Morris have turned Oxford into a world important monument of Victorian stained glass. The great proliferation of Victorian stained glass, which was to restore Oxford as a city of stained glass, left little opportunity for the expression of a modern idiom. A notable exception is the chapel in Nuffield College, where John Piper's windows help create the atmosphere for contemplation that the medieval masters would well have understood.

Almost more than any other city in England, Oxford has experienced an evolving stained glass tradition which has contributed to establishing a city of great historical beauty.

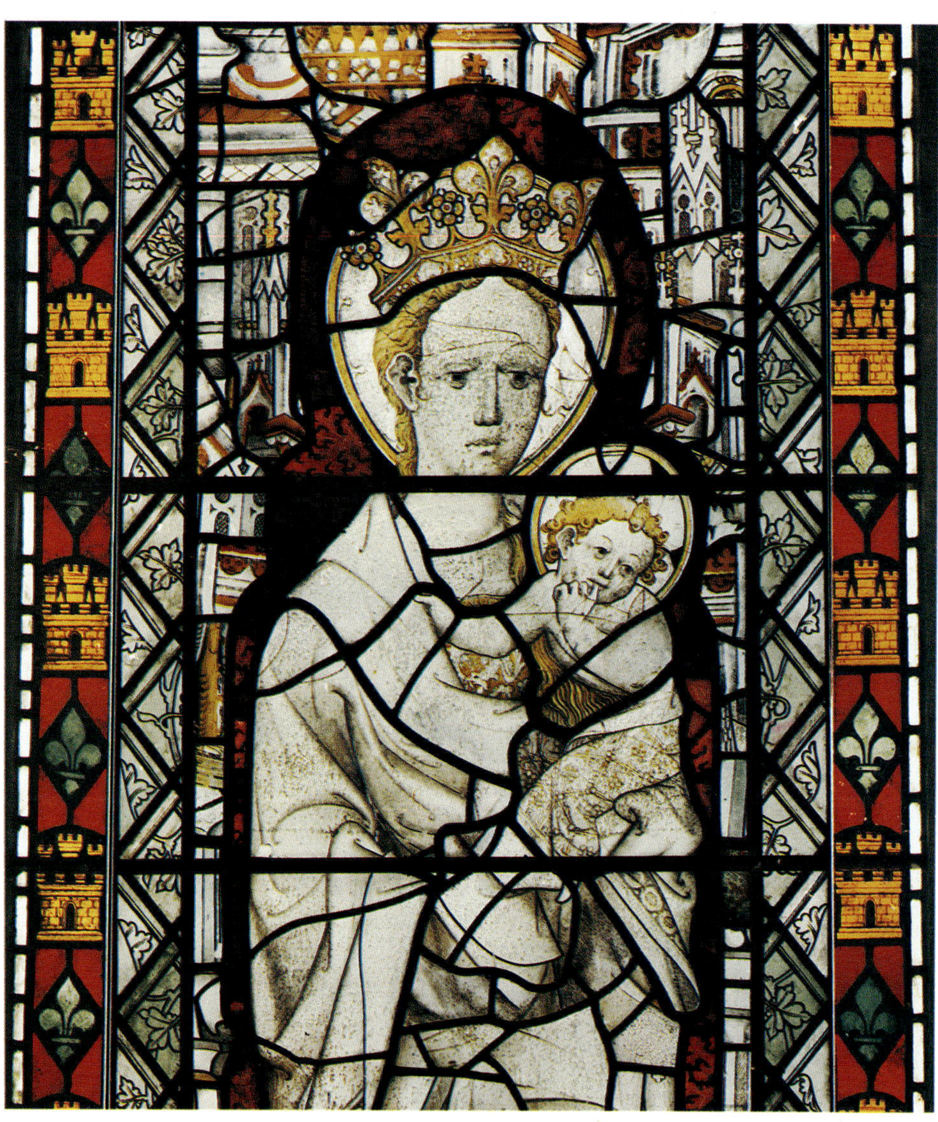

MEDIEVAL GLASS IN OXFORD

The Venerable Bede, writing in the 8th century, describes the use of coloured glass in the windows of Anglo-Saxon churches of the 7th century. Fragments of glass excavated on the site of Bede's monastery retain their bright colour, but show no traces of paint, suggesting that the earliest windows were of a decorative rather than narrative character. Painted glass of the 9th century has been found on the Continent but it is only really in the late 12th century that the history of English glass-painting can be said to begin, with the great collection of windows in Canterbury Cathedral, which spans the transition from Romanesque to Gothic.

Oxford has no 12th-century glass, but in the 13th century the city was transformed into a major academic and intellectual centre, the home of Europe's second great university — following in the footsteps of Paris — and it is from this period that evidence of an important resident community of painters and illuminators survives. Oxford's 13th-century stained glass is of major importance, reflecting the skill and sophistication of the glass-painters who settled in the city to serve the rapidly expanding collegiate community and the large numbers of religious houses. Benedictines, Augustinians, Cistercians, Carmelites, Trinitarians, Franciscans and Dominicans all settled in Oxford in the course of the 13th century. These religious orders, and the buildings they commissioned, have disappeared with little or no trace, but a memory of them remains in some of the city's place names such as Blackfriars Road and Greyfriars House.

Probably the earliest glass to survive in the city is to be found in the parish church of St Michael at the North Gate. The four figures of St Nicholas, St Edmund of Abingdon, St Michael, and the Virgin and Child, are simply and effectively painted with childlike, innocent

Fig. 1. In the soft modelled style of the late 14th century, the Virgin Mary is presented as a gentle mother, and the child Jesus as a happy baby boy. (Merton College Chapel, window 1)

faces. Each figure is labelled with the remains of an inscription in bold Lombardic capitals that are clear and easy to read. Glass in a similar style can be found outside the city, at Stanton Harcourt and nearby Dorchester Abbey.

Merton College Chapel

Displaying an altogether greater degree of sophistication are the choir windows of Merton College chapel. The Merton windows reflect the considerably greater status and wealth of their patron, with his academic and cosmopolitan connections. The windows were the gift of Henry de Mamesfeld, Fellow of Merton and Chancellor of the University, and are usually dated *c.* 1289-96.

In terms of both its architecture and stained glass, Merton College chapel is a building of national importance. In the second half of the 13th century, the narrow lancet window had been superceded by a larger window opening, divided into individual lights, and surmounted by an elaborate pattern formed by a stone web, or tracery. It is this type of window that illuminates the choir of Merton chapel. The new architecture called for new stained glass. The glass-painter abandoned the dark, densely filled medallion window and instead filled the openings with a series of single figures under architectural canopies, far better suited to the tall narrow lights created by the window tracery. The canopies above each figure imitated the gabled architecture of the building itself. The architect, who was now enlivening his wall surface with sculpture and carved ornament, required a better illuminated interior. The glass-painter responded by arranging his figure panels in horizontal bands across the window, alternating with bands of lighter, silvery 'grisaille', panels made of small panes ('quarries') of white glass painted with foliage. In the Merton windows the pieces are leaded in such a way that the foliage gives the impression of winding through a trellis. The side

Fig. 2. St Edmund of Abingdon (1175–1240), as Edmund Rich was educated at Oxford University and returned to teach there. In 1233 he was appointed Archbishop of Canterbury; in 1246 he was the first Oxford don to be canonized, not long before this glass was made. (Church of St Michael at the North Gate, shown on the map, but not entered in the Gazetteer)

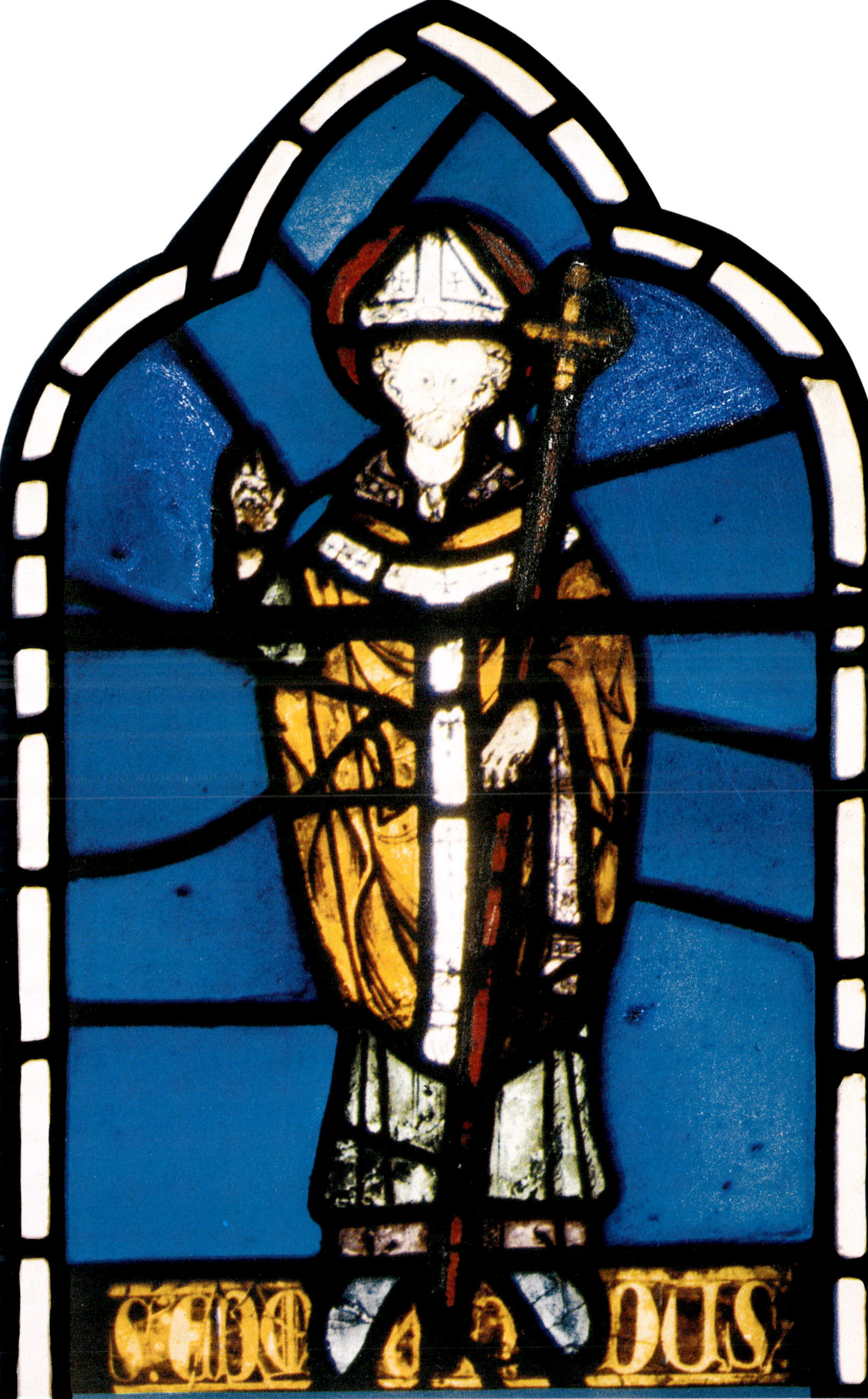

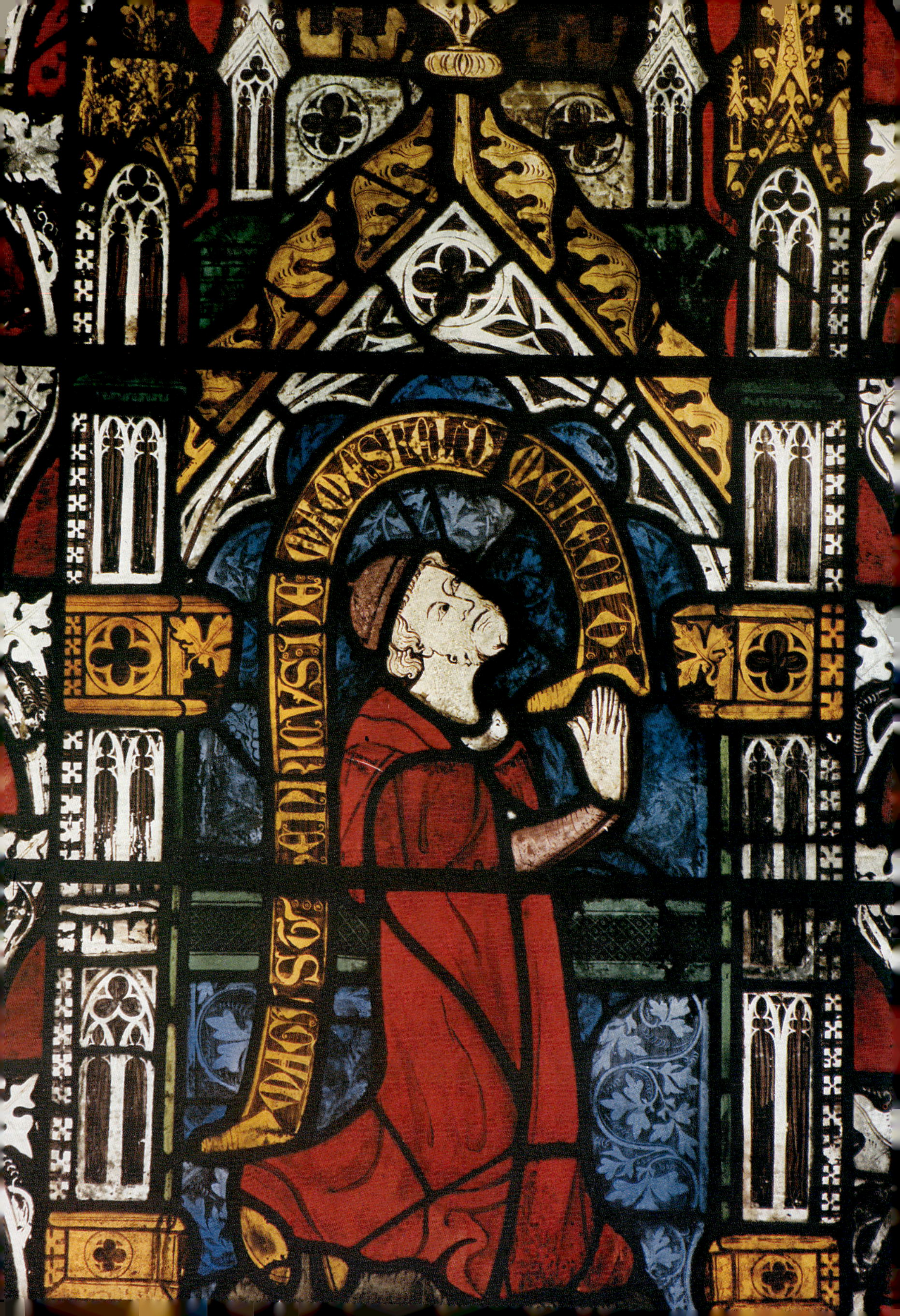

windows of the choir contain one of the earliest and most refined examples of this new kind of Gothic window, and the figure beneath the canopy was to become a standard feature of two centuries of stained glass design.

The Merton figures epitomize the liveliness of English Gothic painting — they are dainty and doll-like, with delicately painted faces and refined gestures. Each one is framed by a canopy and stands against a deeply coloured background decorated with trails of finely executed naturalistic foliage. This is best seen in the panels of grisaille, which depict recognizable leaf forms such as oak, maple and ivy. It is one of the earliest examples of the use of naturalistic rather than conventionalized leaf forms in stained glass, and this extends into the border decoration, where climbing foliage and heraldic devices (castles and fleurs-de-lis) are used in alternate windows. Heraldry, another major innovation in the decorative repertoire of the late 13th century, and one which reflects the increasingly important influence of the secular world, is an important motif in the Merton windows. Apart from the borders, it also features as one of the principal elements in the decoration of the great window over the altar, where it dominates the rose motif in the apex.

One of the most memorable features of these choir windows is the appearance no less than twenty-four times of the donor, Henry de Mamesfield. The prominence of the donor figure, another motif introduced in the 13th century, is a reminder of the growing importance of the individual in the commissioning of works of art. The Merton College chapel windows represent one of the earliest and best preserved examples of the consistent application of all these new principles of window design. The quality of the workmanship is exceptional and the windows have benefited from sensitive restoration.

Fig. 3. Portrait of Henry de Mamesfeld, great donor and Fellow of Merton College, late 13th century. Henry's 'portrait' in the choir windows is unlikely to have been drawn from life — portraiture in the modern sense only began to develop at the very close of the Middle Ages. None the less, the glass-painter has created a striking image of a man at the height of his career. (Merton College Chapel, window 5)

Christ Church Cathedral

The early 14th-century glass in the tracery of the window in the Lucy Chapel of Christ Church Cathedral introduces another aspect of Gothic window decoration, namely the use of grotesque and humorous marginalia. Mixed in with a series of lively figure panels, including the relatively rare depiction of the martyrdom of St Thomas Becket, is a number of fantastic hybrid creatures. This type of 'grotesque', also found in the margins of contemporary illuminated manuscripts, is a significant feature of 14th-century stained glass in Oxford, recurring in the later 14th-century Latin Chapel windows in the Cathedral and in the windows of New College chapel, commissioned at the close of the century.

It is also in the Lucy Chapel that yellow stain, the most important technical innovation of the 14th century, makes its first appearance. Some time around the turn of the 14th century, glass-painters discovered that a silver compound such as silver nitrate would turn yellow when applied and fired on to glass. Until the close of the 15th century, this was to be the only means of adding colour to glass other than in the manufacturing process, and gave the glass-painter a versatile means of adding colour and decoration to even tiny fragments. A head could easily be given golden hair, or a robe a yellow hem, without recourse to the elaborate procedure of cutting and leading individual pieces of coloured glass. This technique was used extensively in the 14th and particularly the 15th centuries and, depending on the method of its application and the skill of the craftsman, could range in colour from a deep orange to a silvery yellow.

In the Latin Chapel, Christ Church Cathedral can claim some of the most important glass of the second quarter of the 14th century. The artists who created these figures, shared with their contemporaries working on manuscripts and murals an interest in the creation of an illusion of three-dimensional space in a two-dimensional

Fig. 4. This 14th-century quatrefoil in the Lucy Chapel shows St Augustine of Canterbury preaching to a group of monks and laymen, one of whom appears to be asleep. The monk in the foreground is taking notes. (Christ Church Cathedral, window 8)

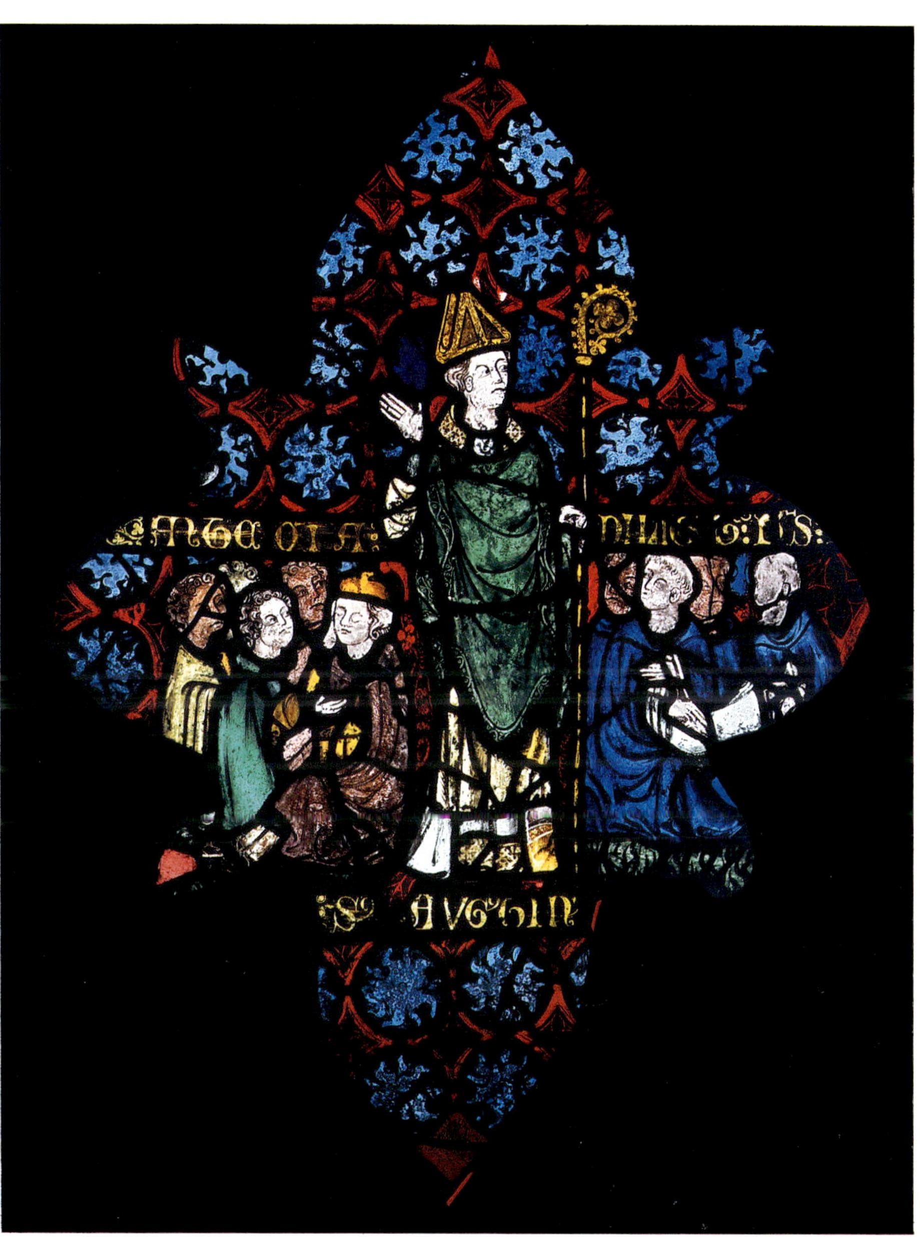

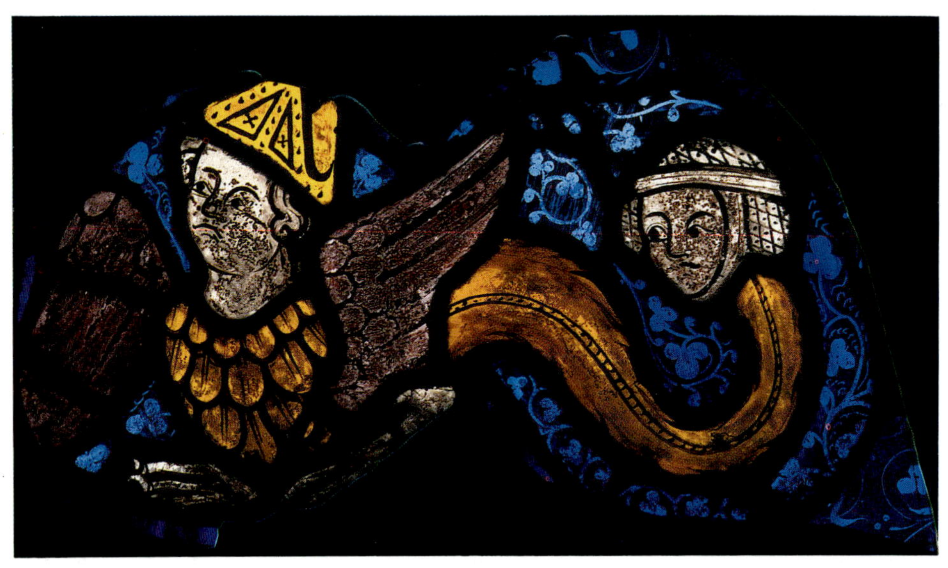

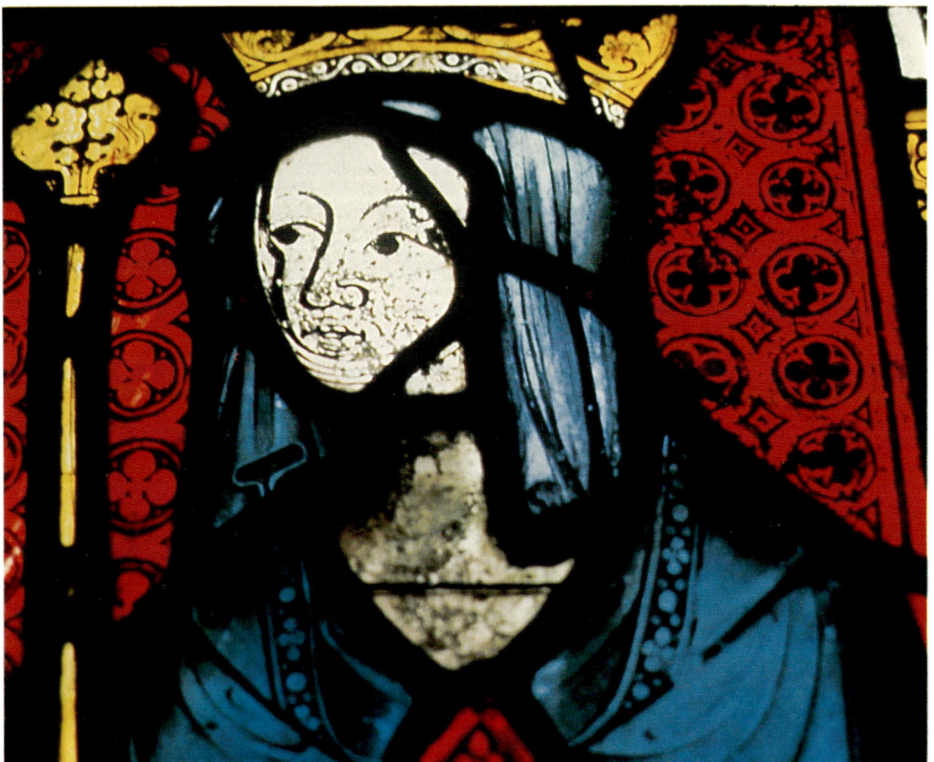

medium. This is particularly true of the canopies, especially of windows 24 and 26, to which the painter has added flying buttresses. This experiment in painterly perspective anticipates later developments at New College. The figures placed under these remarkable canopies are tall and graceful, with rather a pronounced swaying stance.

New College Chapel

In the late 14th-century glazing of New College chapel, Oxford can boast a monument of international importance. The glass was commissioned by one of the most powerful and important figures of the late 14th century, William of Wykeham, Bishop of Winchester (1366-1404) and Chancellor of England to Edward III and Richard II. Dating from the 1380s, a period for which relatively little stained glass survives, these windows are particularly important. No London work of this period remains, although Wykeham's close proximity to the centre of the royal administration means that the Oxford glass probably gives a good impression of Court taste and the prevailing styles of the day.

One is struck immediately by the huge scale of the New College figures and by the new sense of solidity and monumentality that they convey. They are characterized by large, strongly expressive heads, with bold and even rather coarse features. The simple, linear style of face painting found in earlier Oxford glass has been replaced by a more detailed and modelled approach. Eyes are painted with a heavy upper lid, with pupil and iris carefully delineated. Noses are large, protruding and modelled with a variety of fine lines, while hair is painted in a series of vigorous corkscrew-like curls that give some figures a somewhat startled appearance. Others appear grave and serious, with glowering brow. The female saints are gentler in comparison, with innocent expressions and mild, clear faces.

Fig. 5. *A 14th-century two-headed hybrid figure from the Lucy Chapel ridicules both the secular clergy and womankind. Grotesques, as these hybrid figures were called, were typical of the day in wood-carving and manuscript illumination as well as stained glass. (Christ Church Cathedral, window 8)* **Fig. 6.** *Detail of the head of Hilda, saintly Northumbrian abbess, shows her dressed in monastic habit, her head swathed in the veil and wimple worn by all religious women. The decoration of her crown and sceptre (a reference to her royal lineage) demonstrates the use of yellow stain to enliven small pieces of white glass. (Christ Church Cathedral, window 22)*

The decorative quality of the New College glass is exceptional. The palette is subtle and markedly quieter than the Christ Church colour range. An olive green and purpley red have been introduced and yellow stain is used abundantly, particularly on the diversity of motifs that decorate the white mantles worn by most of the figures. Philip and Simon, for example, wear robes decorated with flying dragons, while those of Bartholomew are decorated with fighting cocks. The backgrounds are powdered with the appropriate initial letters of the figures, sometimes crowned, a most unusual feature. Not all of these initials now accompany the correct figure.

Eleven different canopy designs have been counted and it is the canopies that are one of the most singular and attractive aspects of this glass, for they display a considerable degree of architectural perspective. The canopies are topped with turrets and pinnacles of remarkably rounded form, from which fly jaunty little pennants. The tentative beginnings made in the Christ Church Latin Chapel have come to fruition.

It is at New College that we first encounter an identifiable artist. The Steward of the Hall's record book and Wykeham's household records relating to both New College and Winchester (his other educational collegiate foundation) reveal that the artist in charge of the glazing schemes at both was Thomas Glasier (or Glasyer) of Oxford. He was sufficiently esteemed to be invited to dine with the Fellows of New College on a number of occasions and was depicted together with the architect, carpenter and clerk of works at the base of the east window of Winchester College (a 19th-century copy has replaced the medieval original). It is at just this period that the medieval artist begins to emerge from obscurity, attaining a greater degree of social status in his relationship with his patron.

The transition from Thomas Glasier's surviving New College figures to the far softer and more painterly figures of All Souls College

Fig. 7. *St John the Evangelist, by Thomas Glasier, 14th century. This gentle figure, once flanking the Crucified Christ, depicts St John the Evangelist, the apostle to whom Christ entrusted his mother, the Virgin Mary. The posture, with one hand pressed to the cheek, is the typically stylized gesture common throughout the Middle Ages. The features of his face are depicted in meticulous detail — every delicate hair of the brow is visible, while a tiny curl escapes from the otherwise neat arrangement of the hair — a remarkable departure from earlier simpler painting styles. (New College Chapel, window 6)*

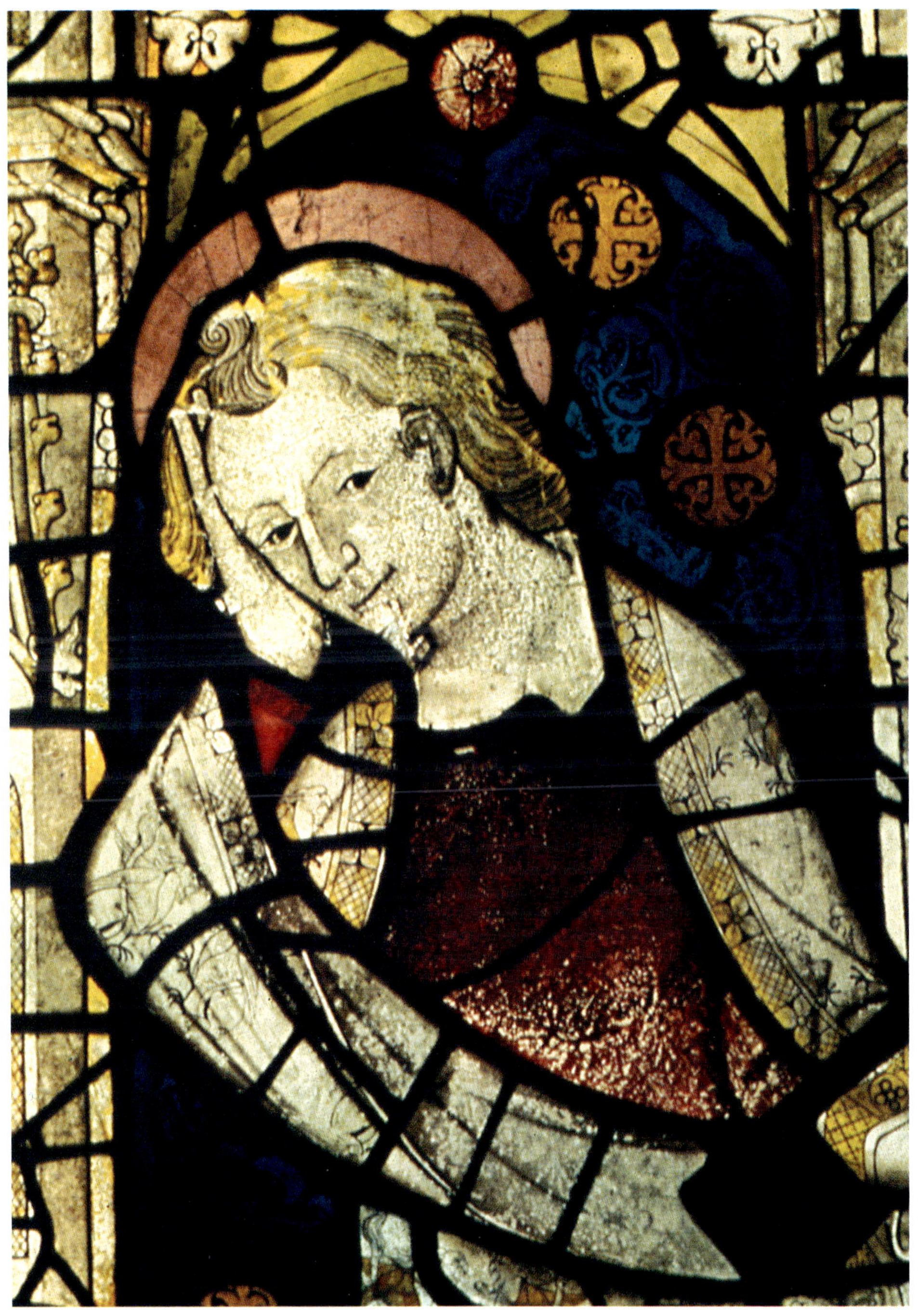

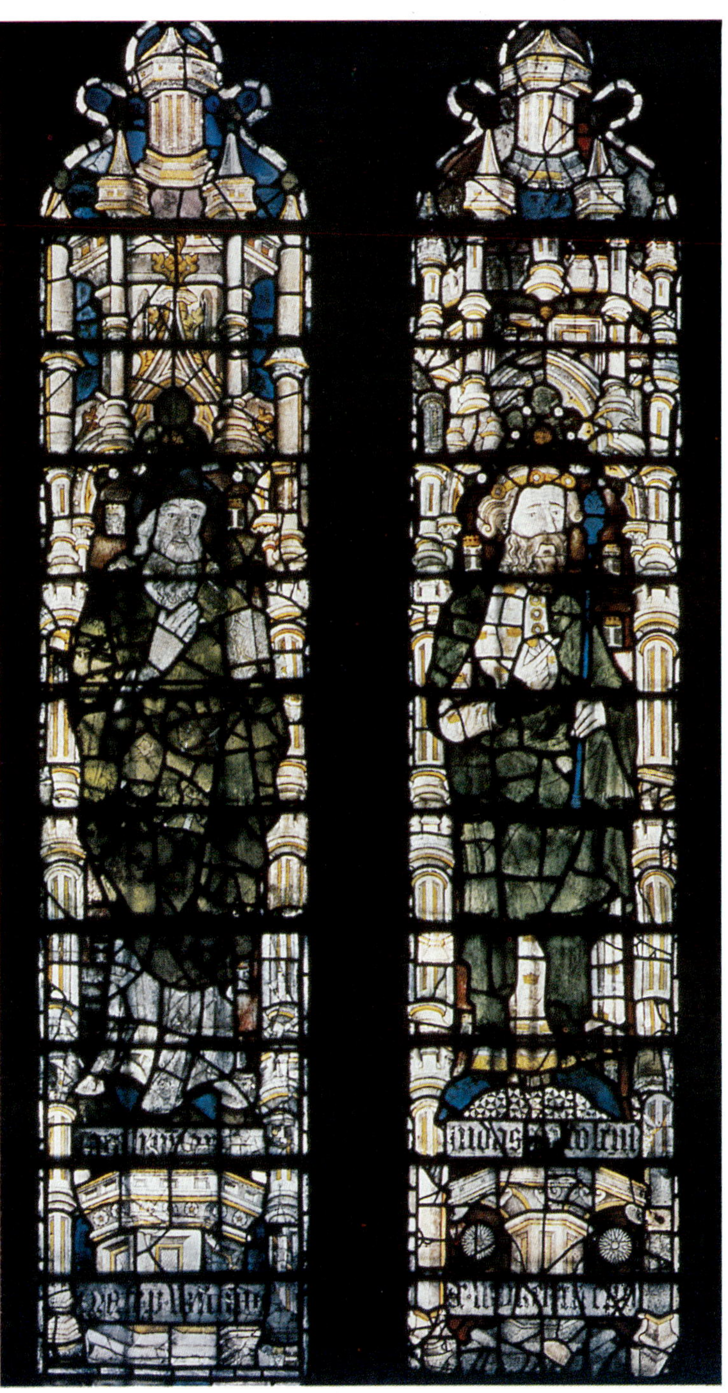

was made in the last decade of the 14th century, and probably within the Glasier workshop. The loss of the original Jesse Tree window at New College (removed in the 18th century) makes this difficult to chart, but some impression of the subtle evolution can be gained from the remains of another Glasier product, the beautiful but sadly curtailed figures now placed in the window over the altar in Merton College chapel. The treatment of hair retains the wild corkscrew character of the New College prophets, but the gentle, contemplative faces anticipate the work of John Glasier at All Souls. Thomas Glasier is known to have had a son and it is tempting to surmise that this was the man who led a younger group of artists within the New College workshop, and who was to be called to work as the leader of his own workshop at Henry Chichele's All Souls College.

All Souls College Chapel

On 13 May 1441 John Glasier was paid for the eight windows of All Souls College chapel and in 1447 he was paid for the principal window of the antechapel. The figures that survive are clearly the heirs of the New College figures, with the modelling technique fully developed. Hair curls gently around the mild and untroubled faces. The figures stand under deeply recessed canopies, the spatial depth emphasized by the receding tiled pavements on which they rest. The plinths under their feet project strongly, an effect which is enhanced by the ribbons of inscription that wind through them.

The figures are all elaborately dressed, particularly the female saints, who wear an assortment of fashionable head-dresses. Although a great deal of white glass is used, the abundance of yellow stain and the ornately patterned backgrounds, painted in imitation of opulent cloth hangings, create a rich and glowing effect. The varied palette of New College has been succeeded by a predominantly red/blue/yellow effect that is typical of so much 15th-century English glass.

Fig. 8. Thomas Glasier's massive New College figures achieve a startling degree of realism. The canopies have a rounded quality and the way in which the figures overlap their frame creates a convincing sense of space, further enhanced by the use of tiled pavements at the feet of each figure. Judas Maccabeus, the figure on the right, stands against a background patterned with the crowned initial letters (capital I) characteristic of the New College windows; Patriarch Moses is on his left. (New College Chapel, window 12)

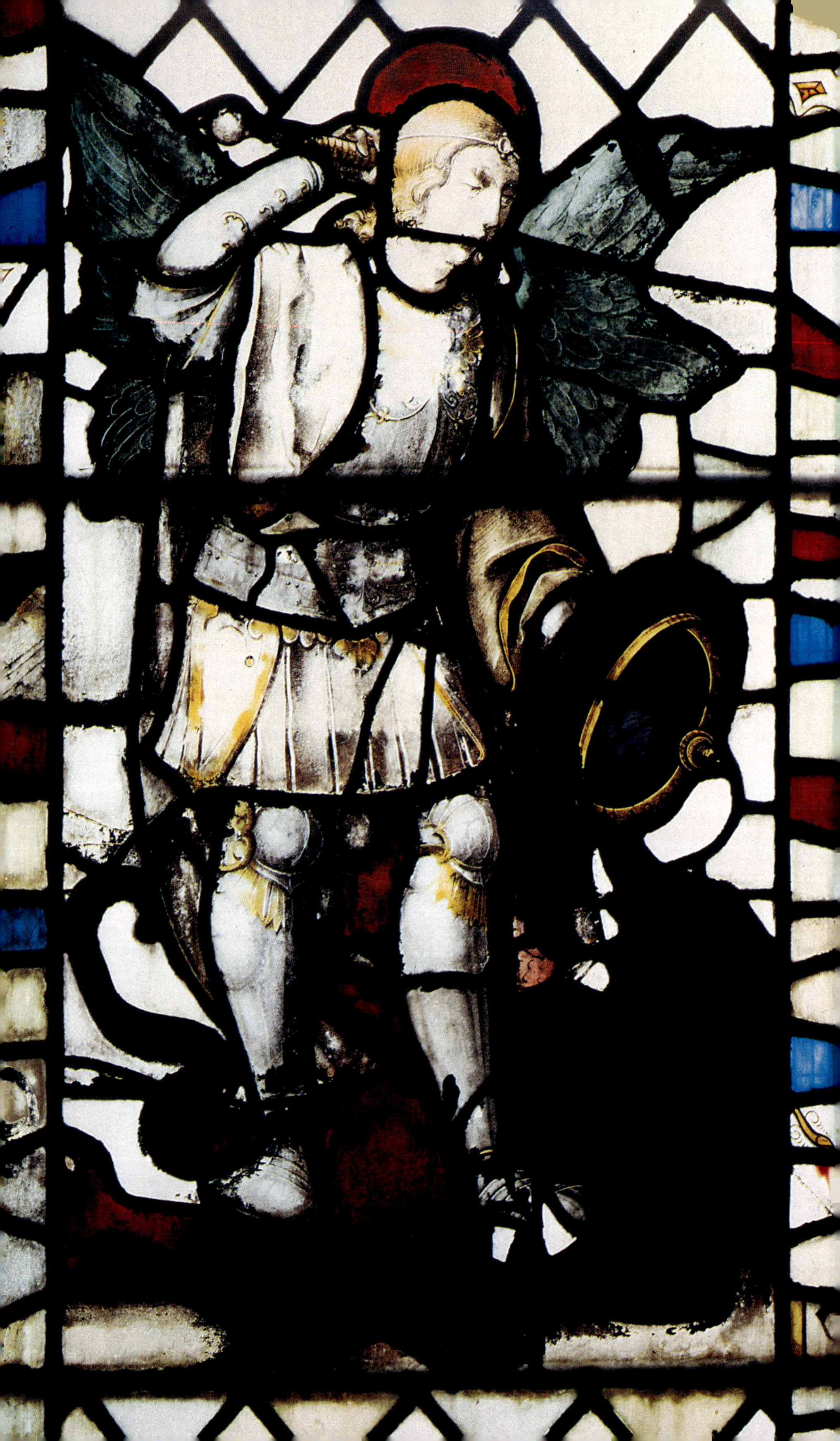

SIXTEENTH-CENTURY GLASS

Important 16th-century schemes survive in Balliol College chapel and in the chapel of The Queen's College. The scheme in the latter, dated 1518, heavily restored though it is, already displays the careful, detailed modelling typical of glass in the new style. Trace lines are reinforced with light modelling washes and layers of stipple, to create a soft, rounded and extremely realistic effect, close to easel painting. The Balliol windows, dating from 1529 and 1530, reveal that the artists responsible were familiar with continental models. The altar window is in two scenes indebted to Albrecht Dürer's Passion series of 1512 (the Agony in the Garden and *Ecce Homo*), made accessible to a great many artists in the form of engravings which circulated throughout the workshops of Europe. One of the notable features of this altar window is its abandonment of the traditional canopy in favour of realistic landscape settings. This is also evident in the St Catherine window. The figures in the other lateral windows no longer preserve their original settings and are now set into plain glazing. One is struck none the less by the monumental and realistic quality of these figures, a quality best appreciated in the better preserved figures such as St Michael and St Margaret.

These fascinating works, however innovative their style, remained true to medieval standards of craftsmanship and in terms of their subject are part of the religious and intellectual milieu of medieval Christendom. It was not the onset of the Renaissance that was to prove a watershed in the history of English stained glass, but the convulsive changes of the Reformation. For the medieval glass-painter the world was never to be the same again.

Fig. 9. This vigorous, muscular figure of the Archangel Michael trampling the vanquished dragon, conveys some impression of the high quality of the 16th-century glass at Balliol. (Balliol College Chapel, window 6)

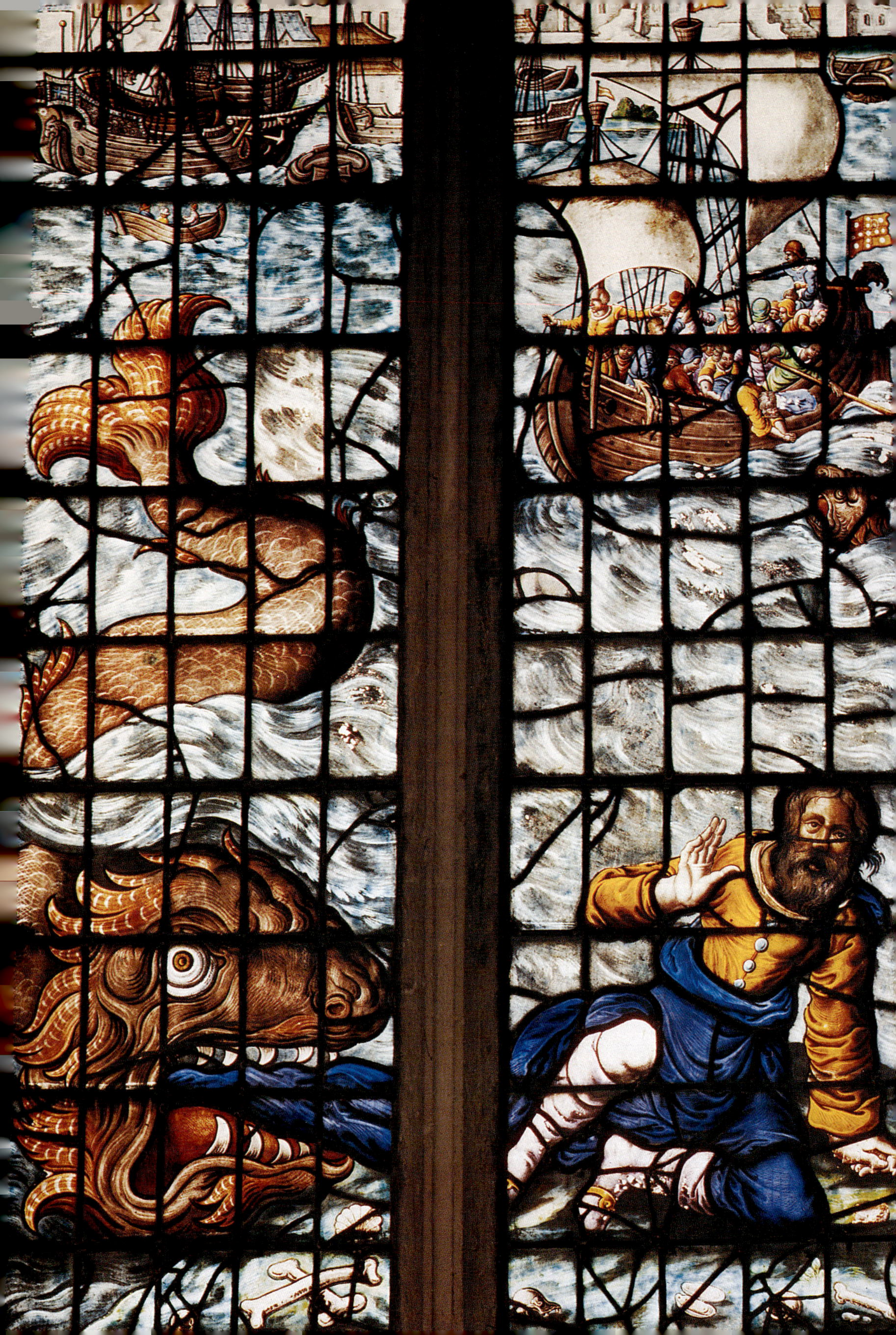

THE REFORMATION AND SEVENTEETH-CENTURY GLASS

The Reformation and Dissolution of the Monasteries (1536-40) brought to an end a considerable period of prosperity and achievement for glaziers working in Oxford. For its size, the city probably had more religious houses than anywhere else in England and these institutions required a constant supply of painted windows. There was still a demand for repairs and some secular commissions, but new ecclesiastical work came abruptly to a halt, removing the greater part of the glass-painter's livelihood. Not only were many foundations suppressed, but Royal Injunctions of 1547 and 1559 laid down that any image which might potentially encourage idolatry should be removed. This resulted in the destruction of a certain amount of glass, and the accounts of New College, for example, show expenditure on window repairs which exactly correspond to these years. It seems likely, though, that it was only particularly provocative images, such as the Crucifixion, that were removed. Certainly enough images remained for Robert Horne, Bishop of Winchester, who was Visitor to the College, to order further destruction in 1567. On similar visitations to Trinity in 1561 and 1566 he ordered the removal of 'Crosses, Sensars and such lyke fylthie Stuffe', which had been installed on the foundation of the college in 1555 during the brief return to orthodox Catholicism in the reign of Queen Mary. Despite these attacks there is no record of extensive reglazing at New College and it is likely that this reflects the situation within the University of Oxford generally.

But for monastic foundations the damage caused was colossal. Gloucester, Durham and Canterbury Colleges vanished entirely and

Fig. 10. Jonah and the Whale, by Abraham van Linge, who signed and dated this window in 1641. By this time his style had become broad and emphatic, unlike the delicate, lively panels he painted for Lincoln College ten years earlier. He painted a Jonah and the Whale for each of these chapels. Although the glass for University College was painted in 1641, it was not installed until 1666, after the Civil War, when the chapel was completed. (University College Chapel, window 10)

the lands and endowments of Osney Abbey, Rewley Abbey and St Frideswide's Priory were made over to Christ Church, then known as Cardinal College after its founder Cardinal Wolsey. A number of monastic colleges were incorporated in newer foundations and their endowments transferred to Oxford University. The Dissolution, which might have seriously threatened the University in fact, on the whole, led to a strengthening of its resources and Henry VIII could 'judge no land better bestowed than that which is given to our Universities, for by their maintenance our Realm will be governed when we are dead and rotten'.

This transfer of resources can be discerned in the career of Robert King, last Abbot of Osney. On its suppression he was made the first bishop of Oxford and shortly afterwards transferred, with Dean and Chapter, to Christ Church where the college chapel became the Cathedral. Besides the enrichment of existing colleges, the University actually expanded with the foundation of Trinity and St John's in 1555, followed by Jesus in 1571. Fifty years earlier a programme of building on this scale would have provided attractive opportunities for stained glass artists, but the prevailing religious climate of the second half of the 16th century allowed little scope for anything more than modest heraldic work.

It was not until the building boom in Oxford during the first half of the next century that painted windows could again be installed without arousing accusations of idolatry. The first new college to be built in the 17th century was Wadham, which was erected in a single building programme between 1610 and 1613. Documentary evidence shows that three artists painted panels for the chapel. A local man, Robert Rudland, was paid for work in 1613 and 1614 and is likely to have been responsible for four of the prophets on the north side. The figures of Christ, the Apostles, and St Paul and St Stephen on the south side, one of which is dated 1616, are all probably by Lewis Dolphin who is represented at Hatfield House and elsewhere. The remaining prophets on the north side are in the style of Bernard van Linge who is known to have carried out the east window in 1622. Bernard was a native of Emden (Germany), who came to London in 1621, after four years in Paris. His only other work seems to have been one of the chapel side windows of Lincoln's Inn (*c.* 1623-6) and he is known to have returned to Emden by 1628. The window over the altar at Wadham is partly based on a series of engraved book illustrations by Martin de Vos, printed in Antwerp in 1595, and is largely painted in enamel pigments. The introduction of this technique radically altered the appearance of painted windows. Not only was the available range of colours quite different from pot-metal glass used during the Middle Ages, but the artist could paint on regular rectangles of clear glass. This method remained in use until the early 19th century and can be studied better in Oxford than anywhere else.

The windows of Wadham College chapel, and in particular the Passion series in the altar window, amply demonstrate the change in attitude to the beautification of churches that had taken place during the reign of James I. Images were again tolerated and the prospects of stained glass artists, in company with other craftsmen, were much improved. Perhaps encouraged by this new climate of opinion, Bernard van Linge's brother, Abraham, now appears on the scene. He is likely to have arrived in Oxford before his brother's departure and stylistic evidence shows that he painted the windows for the chapel of Lincoln College, which was built between 1629 and 1631. As at Wadham, prophets and apostles face each other across the stalls, while the altar window is filled with representations of Antitypes from the New Testament paired with the Types from the Old Testament, which were thought to prefigure them. Thus the Ascension is paired with the Ascent of Elijah, and the Last Supper with the Passover. The scenes are painted in light and brilliant colours with considerable vivacity, in contrast to the dark, static figures in the Wadham altar window. The upper part of the corresponding window at Lincoln is filled with views of classical buildings inappropriate to the neo-Gothic tracery lights in which they appear. The figures in the side windows are far more at home standing under canopies with angels above them holding shields. Their treatment must be a deliberate allusion to medieval stained glass and harks back to pre-Reformation liturgical practices. The glazing of Lincoln chapel exactly coincides with the High Church revival of Archbishop William Laud, ex-President of St John's, who became Chancellor of Oxford in 1630 and shortly afterwards Archbishop of Canterbury. As chief advisor to Charles I, he enjoyed the King's support in reviving church ceremony which he enforced through injunctions and visitations. A tide of liturgical rearrangement and beautification of college chapels swept through Oxford and Puritanism was forced on to the defensive. Dean Duppa of Christ Church, a keen supporter of the Laudian revival, introduced his views on ritual in the Cathedral and enthusiastically refitted the interior with panelling, screens and glass. Abraham van Linge supplied a window of Jonah before Ninevah, which he signed, and the figure of Bishop King in the south aisle. He must also have done the windows in the north transept of which only the tracery lights remain. The whole decade was a particularly busy one for him, since he carried out major commissions for Queen's in 1635, Balliol in 1637 and University College in 1641. It is difficult to appreciate his windows at Queen's as they are no longer in the building for which they were intended. Originally designed for three light windows with small tracery lights above, they were converted in the 18th century to fit single, large round-headed openings. At Balliol, and above all at University College, his brilliant colours and love of exotic and often amusing detail can be seen to perfection. Although prolific, he had no monopoly of work in Oxford. Richard Greenbury, a painter in oils, was paid in 1632 for the large number of monotone saints in the antechapel of Magdalen. He may also have done the Last Judgement that is known to have been in the west window there, but has been lost.

Although there must have been more early 17th-century glass in Oxford than now survives, some perhaps by artists other than those already mentioned, the opportunity for further work was cut short by the outbreak of the Civil War in 1642. Oxford became the headquarters of Charles I and was only saved from extensive damage by a negotiated surrender after the siege of 1646. Inevitably the embellishment of college chapels came to a halt as the High Church movement yielded to Puritanism. Fortunately, the city was spared serious iconoclasm, although a certain amount of destruction took place after Oliver Cromwell's defeat of Charles I at the Battle of Worcester. At Christ Church, one of the intended canons, 'furiously

Fig. 11. This scene of the Agony in the Garden is part of a Passion sequence in the lower part of the window, while the upper part has scenes from the Old Testament. The revival of glass-painting at Oxford in the 17th century began when Wadham College decided to employ Bernard van Linge to paint the east window of the chapel in 1622. He had just arrived in England from Paris and brought with him a knowledge of continental painting styles. (Wadham College Chapel, window 1)

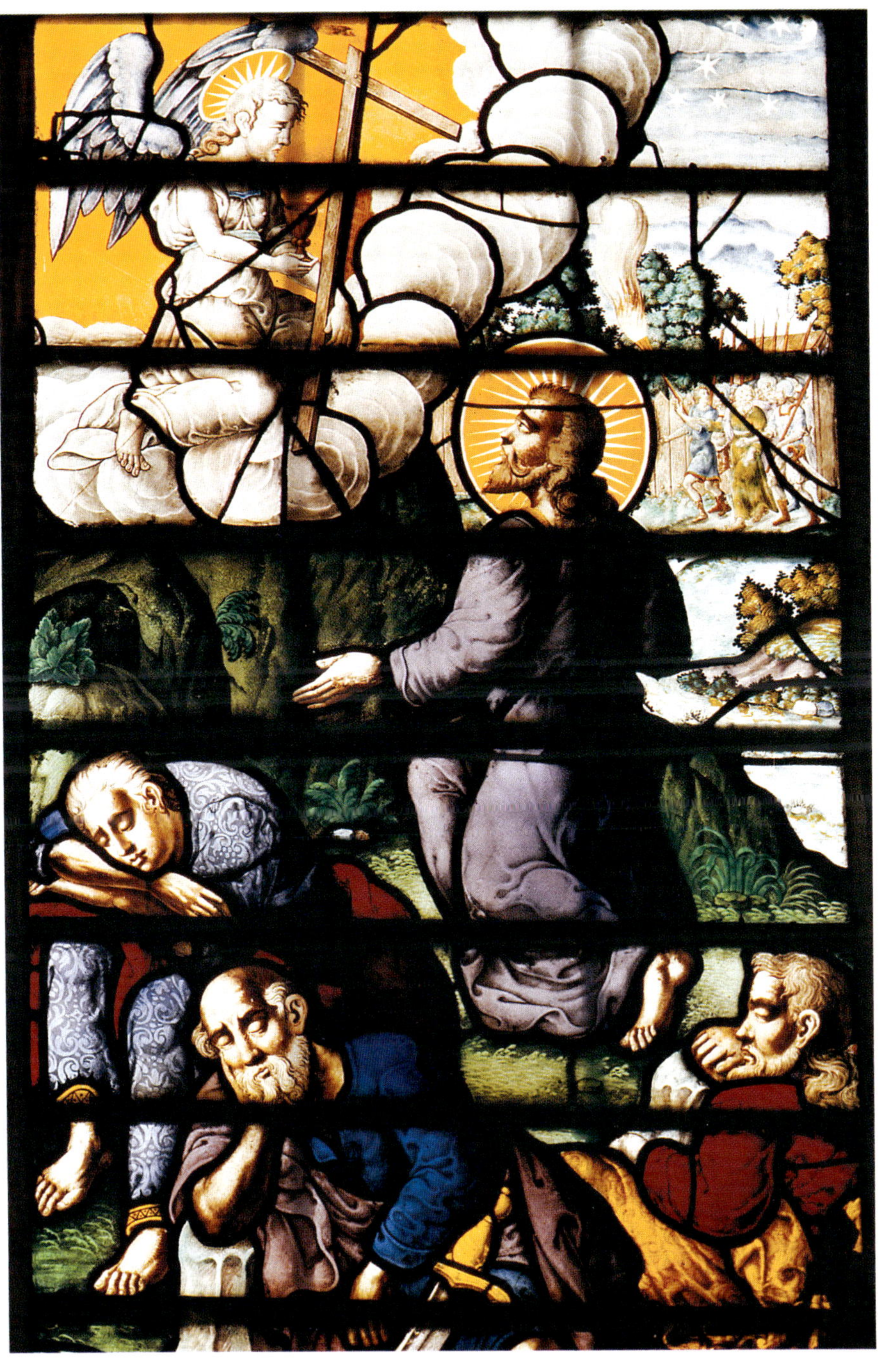

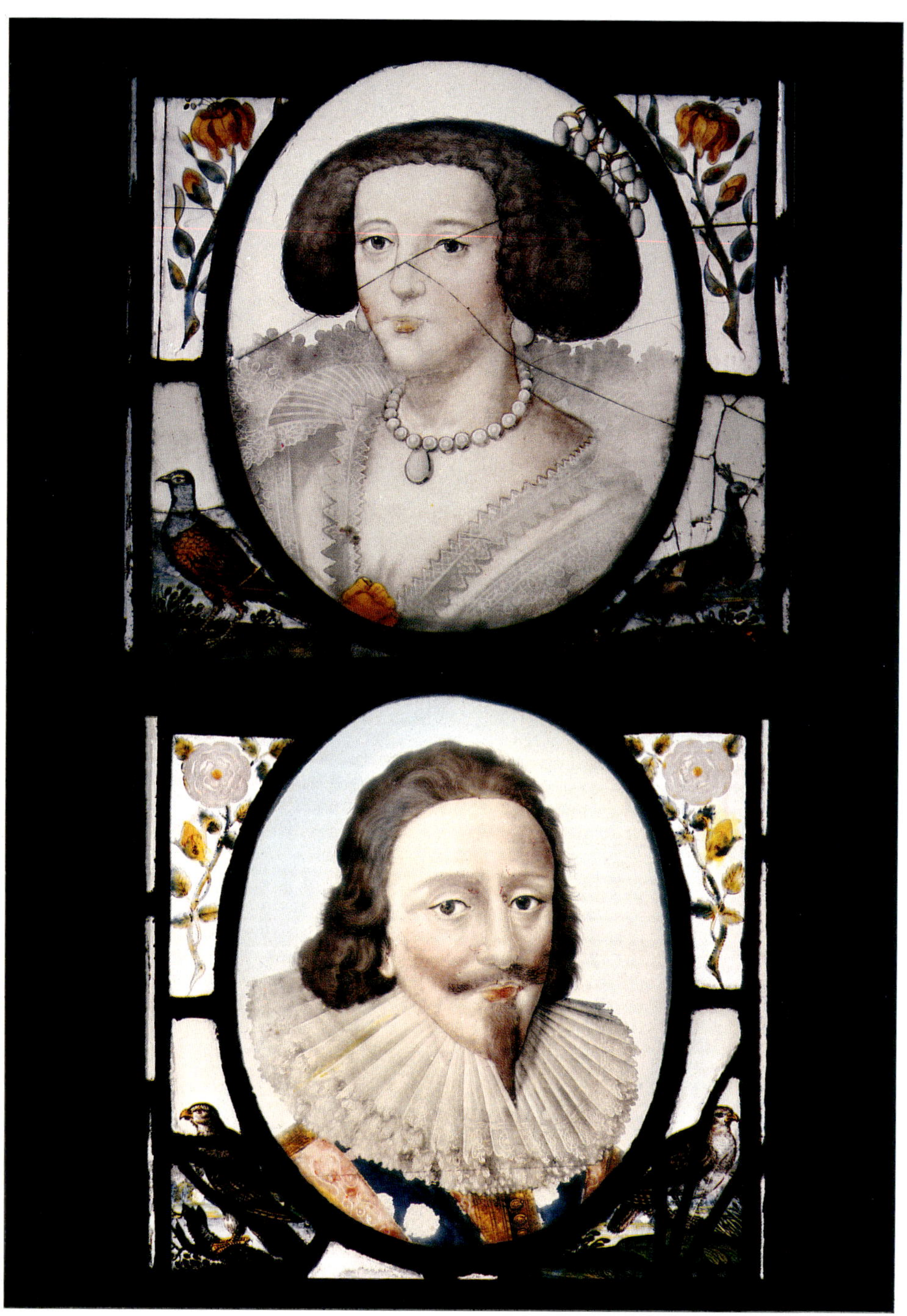

stamped upon' some of the glass, but the Parliamentarian soldiers seem to have admired the 'painted idolatrous windows'. The van Linge portrait of Bishop King owed its survival to the foresight of his family, who temporarily removed the window to safety.

Abraham van Linge's last known windows were those he did for University College chapel in 1641, after which there is no record of him. The glass was not installed until the building of the chapel was completed in 1666 and did not include an altar window. Although Anglican ritual, prayer-books, organs, surplices, and so forth, returned to use on the Restoration of Charles II in 1660, the college did not commission a design until 1682, when they approached Henry Gyles, a native of York, the outstanding glass-painter of the period. Gyles supplied a window for the chapel and another for the college hall, but unfortunately they were all removed in the 19th century and all that survives of his work is a sundial, not located in the public part of the building.

Figs. 12 and 13. Portraits of King Charles I and his Queen, Henrietta Maria, early 17th century, in the oriel window of the Great Hall, Magdalen College.

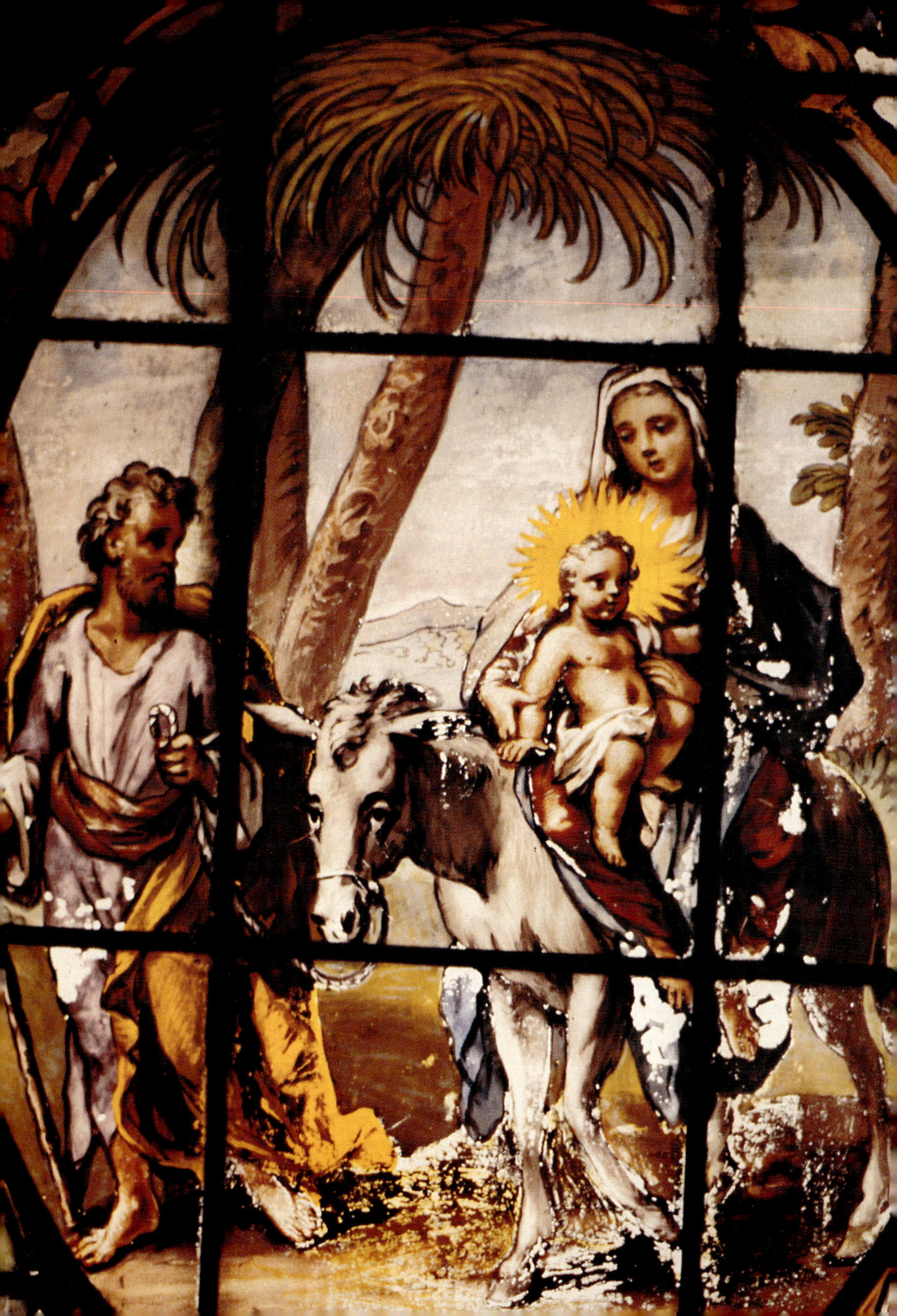

EIGHTEENTH-CENTURY GLASS

Although the 18th century at Oxford has been described as a period of 'distressing somnolency', considerable vigour was shown in building work and most colleges were either added to or rebuilt. A new chapel was built at Queen's College between 1714 and 1719 and, as we have seen, the 17th-century glass was ingeniously reused. The artist chosen to do this work was Joshua Price of Hatton Garden in London, who had been in partnership with his father William until the latter's death in 1709. The only window in the chapel entirely by Joshua is the one above the altar. Regrettably it gives very little idea of the quality of his painting, as it was most unsympathetically restored in the 19th century. Fortunately, the ovals at the top of the Resurrection, Ascension and Last Judgement windows, as well as many skilfully placed cupids' heads, have survived untouched and show his fine Italianate draughtsmanship and warm, unobtrusive colouring.

At Queen's, Joshua Price was faced with the unenviable task of amalgamating glass of different periods into a more or less coherent whole. He carried this out with a meticulous self-effacing concern for the old glass, which is also apparent in the work of his son William, the most significant English glass painter during the middle years of the 18th century. William Price the Younger was first employed at Oxford between 1735 and 1740, when he carried out five windows on the south side of the choir at New College chapel. These he filled with figures in niches, standing on pedestals beneath elaborate canopies. Although the glass could not possibly be mistaken for medieval work, a comparison of the painting of the architectural setting of the figures with their 14th-century counterparts in the antechapel shows that Price was doing his best to make his new scheme harmonize with

Fig. 14 Flight into Egypt, designed by Joshua Price, early 18th century. When The Queen's College replaced its medieval chapel, the old glass was saved, and the task of adapting it to the new classical building was entrusted to Joshua Price in about 1717. He filled most of the windows with late medieval glass and 17th-century scenes by Abraham van Linge, but the east window and the better part of two at the west end were made to his own design. He also filled out spaces at the heads of some of the windows with small scenes such as this Italianate Flight into Egypt. (The Queen's College Chapel, window 3)

what was there already. He clearly saw himself carrying on with the medieval work and went to the lengths of using small pieces of medieval glass in his own windows.

Price's skills were clearly appreciated in Oxford: he was employed at Wadham in 1742 and Magdalen in 1745-6. He restored the van Linge altar window in Wadham chapel and did it with such skill that it is virtually impossible to identify his work. At Magdalen College chapel he supplied two windows either side of the altar but these were taken out in the 19th century and no record survives of what they looked like.

William Price's stately and graceful figures in the chapel of New College, with their rich colouring, gaze across the choir at further tiers of figures by a second remarkable artist. Although they stand in similar architectural niches, their powerful and brilliant colours, at times verging on the vulgar, could not be more different. A contemporary wrote:

> 'Ye colours, that th'unway sight amaze,
> And only dazzle in the noontide blaze!'

These windows were painted in 1765 and 1774 by William Peckitt, a self-taught glass-painter from York. Peckitt's figures of Christ, the Virgin and the Twelve Apostles, originally made for the west window of the antechapel in 1765, were later moved to the north side of the choir where they joined a series of patriarchs and prophets which he painted in 1774. Adam and Eve were shown wearing fig-leaves, but this coverage proved unacceptable to Victorian taste and they were rather more modestly clothed in the 19th century. Peckitt's earlier figures had not met with the complete approval of the college and so, for the second series, an Italian artist, Biagio Rebecca, was employed to provide the cartoons. The only other glass by Peckitt in Oxford is a

Fig. 15. These graceful late-Baroque figures, with their strong colouring, were designed by William Price the Younger. He filled all the windows on the south side of the choir between 1735 and 1740, replacing the decaying remains of the medieval glazing scheme. He clearly intended his replacements to carry on the general effect of the old glass and so copied the design of the canopies above the figures and the plinths on which they stand. This can be seen when one compares them with Thomas Glasier of Oxford's surviving medieval glass in the antechapel. Price even carried his antiquarian approach to the lengths of reusing small pieces of medieval glass. (New College Chapel, window 5)

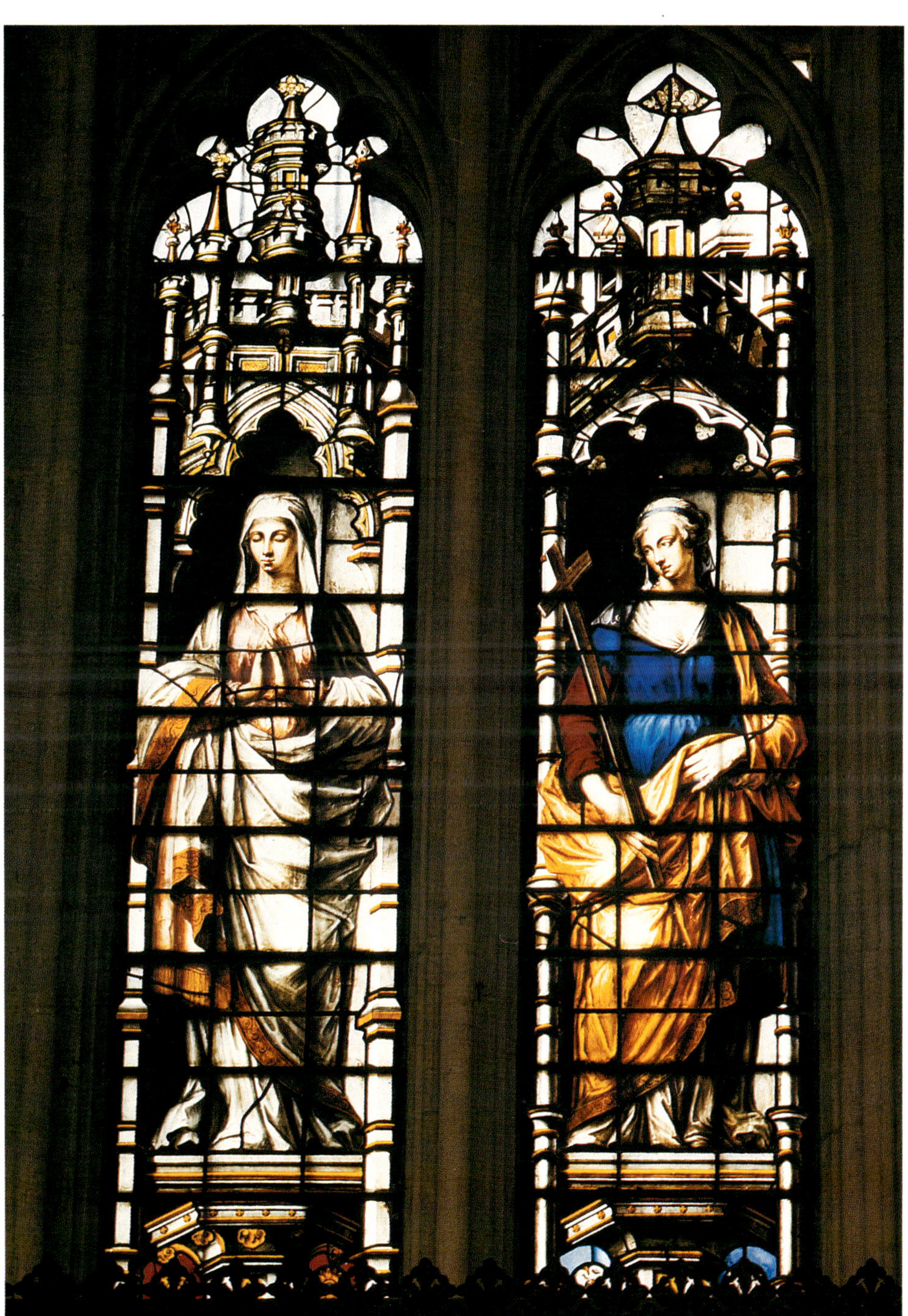

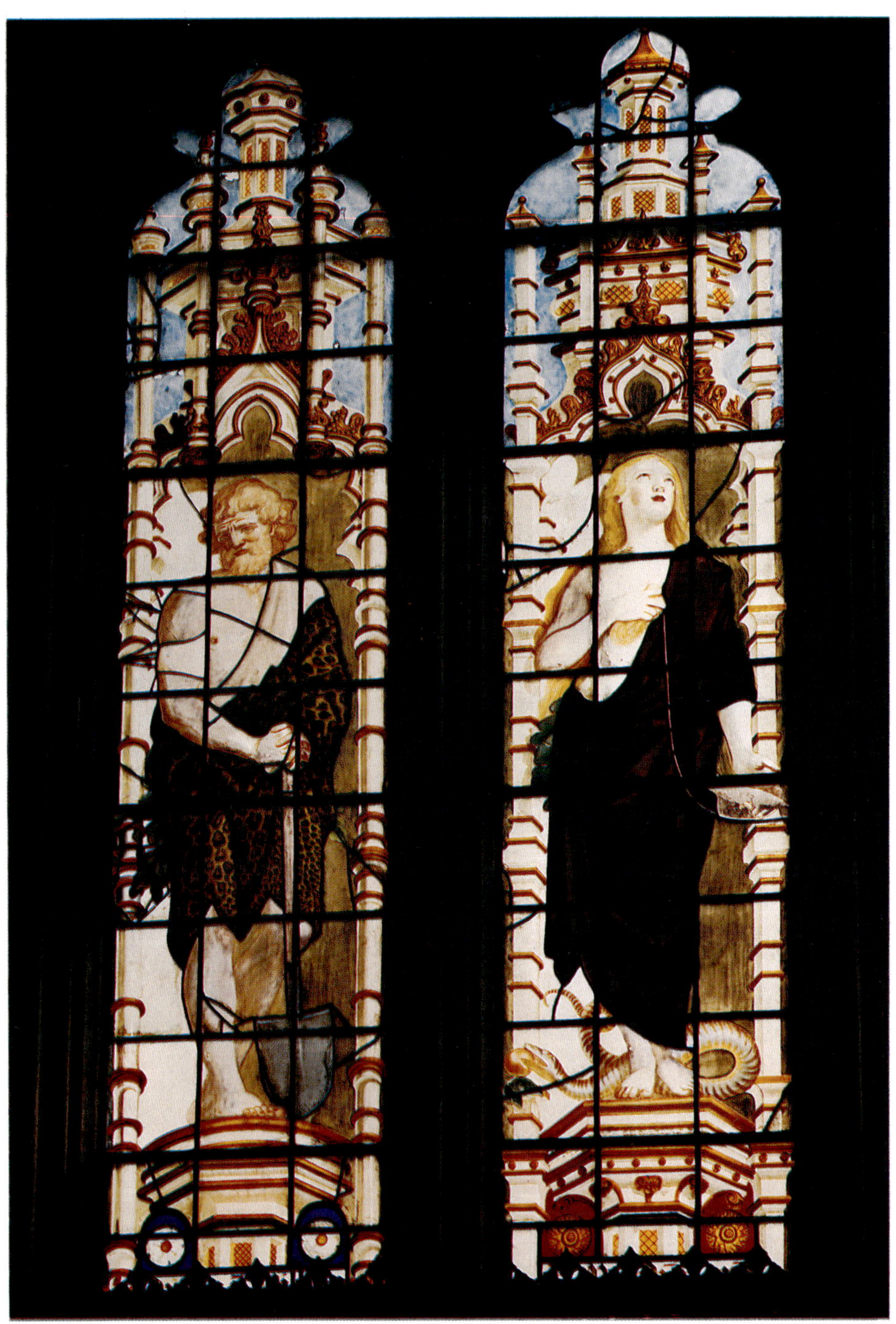

Presentation in the Temple of 1767 at Oriel College chapel. Unfortunately, this was subsequently removed from the window over the altar to a position where it is difficult to see and, as it has lost a certain amount of pigment, its present appearance is not very satisfactory.

For some years after the death of William Price in 1761, Peckitt had a monopoly of the best work available but, long before he himself died in 1795, his paramount position was being challenged by two Irishmen, James Pearson and Thomas Jervais. Pearson was already living in England in 1769 when he accepted his first known commission, to paint the altar window of Ely Cathedral. His only glass in Oxford is the west window of Brasenose College chapel, signed and dated 1776. This shows Christ and the Apostles reset in an entirely 19th-century surround, provided when the glass was moved from the east end. The figures none the less hold their own surprisingly successfully, largely because they possess a statuesque solidity, while their unconventional poses attract attention. St Luke, for example, stands on one foot, legs crossed, nonchalantly leaning on his ox, which is his symbol, and looks over his shoulder at the viewer, with his hand on his hip. The artist responsible for this unexpected image was John Hamilton Mortimer, an important figure in the English Romantic Movement, who provided the original designs for Pearson.

A fitting conclusion to an account of enamel-painted glass in Oxford is the great west window in the chapel of New College. This was the work of Thomas Jervais, who had arrived from Ireland in about 1770. The subjects chosen were the Virtues, who stand in a row across the bottom of the window, and above them the Nativity, after Correggio, which fills the whole of the upper part. The cartoons were supplied by Sir Joshua Reynolds who had completed the figure of Religion, a full-length and life-size oil on canvas, by the autumn of

Fig. 16. The pale elegant figures of Adam and Eve wear soulful, penitent expressions after their expulsion from the Garden of Eden. They were painted by William Peckitt in 1774 after designs provided by an Italian, Biagio Rebecca. Their robes were painted on in the 19th century by a more prudish generation. (New College Chapel, window 14)

1777. As models, he is said to have used various society beauties, amongst them Mrs Sheridan, who also posed for the Virgin in the Nativity. Sir Joshua included portraits of himself and Jervais as shepherds. The installation of the window was not completed until 1783 and it immediately provoked controversy. Thomas Warton composed an eulogy in which he wrote:

> 'Reynolds, tis thine, from the broad window's height,
> To add new lustre to religious light'.

Sir Horace Walpole praised the window when he saw it exhibited in London but criticized the contrast between the pale 'washy Virtues' and the darkness of the Nativity above them. Lord Torrington was rather more outspoken: 'These twisting emblematical Figures appear to me half-dressed languishing Harlots'.

There is no doubt that Walpole's criticism was justified, even when the background of the Virtues was much darker, as it was when he first saw the glass. Nowadays we are inclined to doubt whether it is appropriate to produce a window which was effectively a transparent oil-painting. Contemporaries do not seem to have been troubled by this question and we can best approach it today by accepting the conventions of the technique on its own terms and appreciating its qualities, such as the exquisite delicacy of the heads of the Virtues. This window was the last and by far the most ambitious of its type to be executed in Oxford, and must surely have been the finest anywhere in England during the late 18th century. Although the pictorial tradition of enamel-painting continued after 1800, it was soon superceded by the revival of medieval stained glass techniques that accompanied the triumph of the Gothic Revival.

Fig. 17. *The Nativity was once a controversial window — when it was first exhibited in London, by artificial light, it was much admired, but many were disappointed when it was installed in the west window. Sir Joshua Reynolds, who designed it, included a portrait of himself as one of the shepherds. He is seen looking out of the window towards us. Beside him is Thomas Jervais, who painted the glass between 1775 and 1785. (New College Chapel, window 9)*

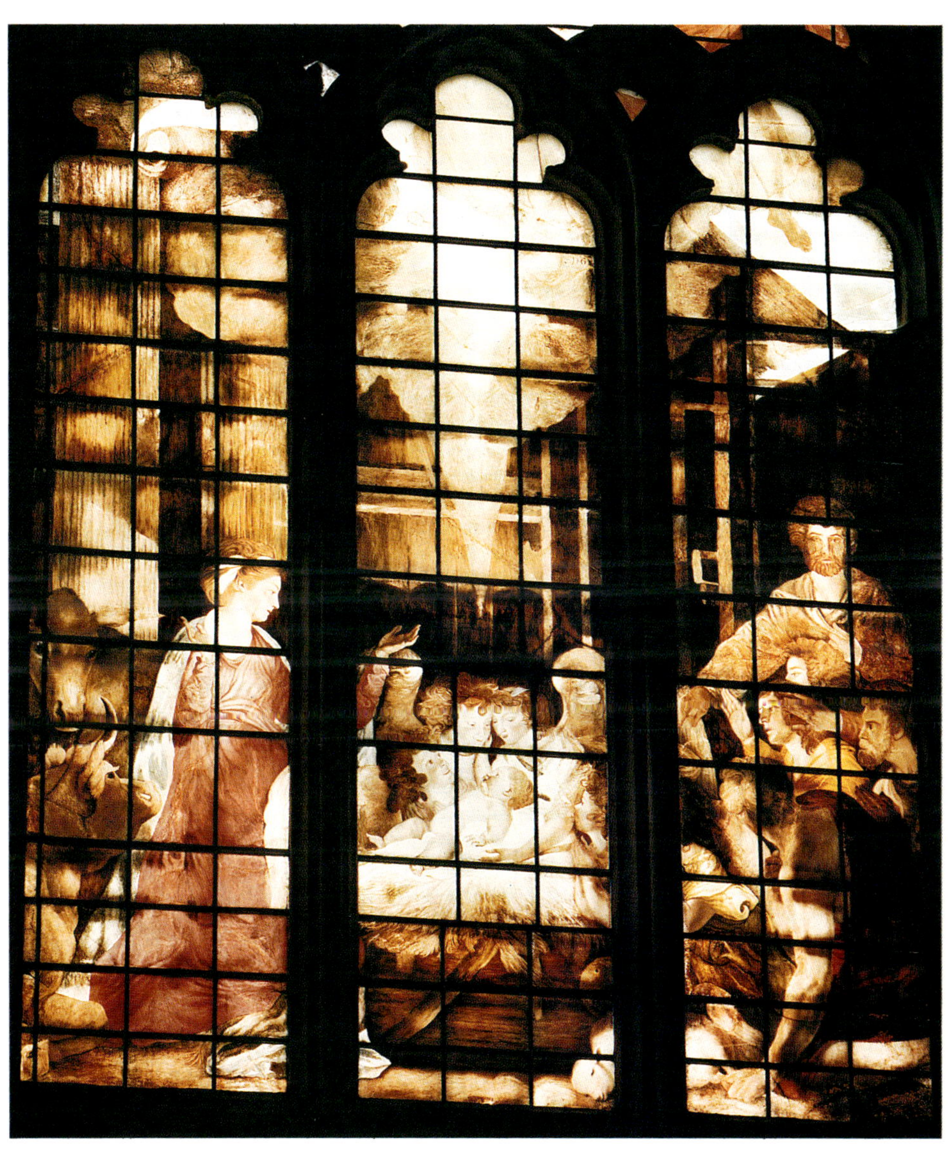

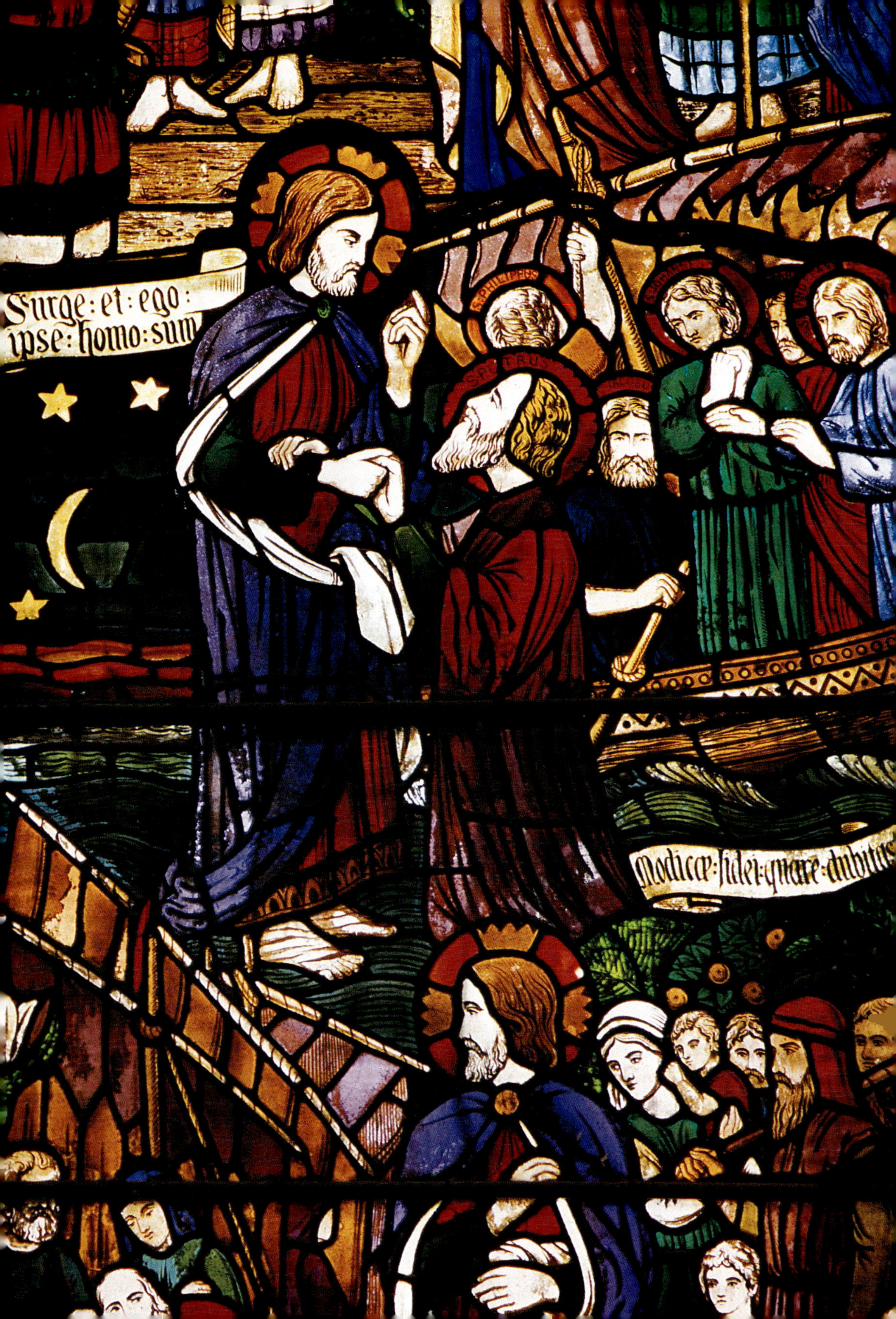
Surge: et: ego:
ipse: homo: sum
S. PETRUS
Modicæ: fidei: quare: dubitas

NINETEENTH-CENTURY VICTORIAN REVIVAL

Oxford has more 19th-century stained glass than of any other period and, in common with the rest of England, its history throughout this period is closely linked with the Gothic Revival in architecture and the applied arts. Oxford can claim two major contributions to the Gothic Revival with significant implications for the art of stained glass. The first was the Oxford Movement, whose leaders (John Henry Newman, Edward Bouverie Pusey and John Keble) were all clergymen educated at Oxford University and whose aim was to reintroduce the Catholic pre-Reformation tradition into the English Church. The Oxford Movement gave a stimulus to all the ecclesiastical arts, not least stained glass, which was regarded as an archetypally medieval art-form, an essential ingredient in the re-creation of an authentically medieval atmosphere, whether in 'restored' ancient buildings or in new buildings in the Gothic style. Oxford's other contribution was through the Pre-Raphaelite artists Edward Burne-Jones and William Morris, both educated at the University, whose work was to revolutionize the visual world of the later Victorian period.

At the beginning of the 19th century, stained glass was stylistically and technically far removed from the great traditions of the Middle Ages, continuing the enamel techniques and painterly traditions of Peckitt and Price. Oxford has only a handful of 19th-century windows in this earlier mould. Eginton's windows in the chapel of New College (1820-1) show no appreciable attempt at imitation of Gothic work. In their windows in Wadham College chapel (1838), Betton & Evans, a studio responsible for early restorations of medieval glass, particularly

Fig. 18. Christ calls St Peter and his brother from their fishing and gives St Peter his hand when the saint attempts to walk on the water. The Irish artist James Rogers seems to have designed only a few windows in the 1860s, but this Life of St Peter is one of the most accomplished windows of its date. Like Burne-Jones' St Frideswide window, it presents several narrative scenes in a continuous design unbroken by ornamental borders or canopy-work. (Christ Church Cathedral, window 11)

at Winchester College, made a more extensive use of pot-metal glass and were less dependent upon enamel-painting. However, it was not until the 1840s that the 'mosaic' method, in which the only colours used are in the glass itself (not applied in the form of enamels), and in which the lead-work has an aesthetic as well as a purely constructional function, became the dominant approach within the craft. This was largely due to the influence of the architect A W N Pugin, the leading figure in the revival of the 'true principles' of the Gothic style. Pugin, himself a Roman Catholic, regarded classicism as a pagan style and published a number of immensely influential works in defence of the Gothic style.

Pugin was a designer of genius in many different media, always basing his work, both technically and stylistically, on authentic medieval designs. The depth of his understanding of the Gothic style can be seen in the two windows which he designed for the church of St Mary the Virgin in the 1840s. Both were given as memorials, an idea in itself reviving the custom of medieval times. Pugin showed the persons commemorated as kneeling figures at the base of each window, echoing the depiction of donors in, for example, the 13th-century windows at Merton College chapel — though Pugin dressed his figures in the ringlets and crinolines, or whiskers and frock-coats of his own time. Above these pious Victorians, the main subjects of each window are drawn in a convincing version of medieval work — the sacred figures wear sumptuously coloured medieval costumes and act out their parts in the religious drama beneath elaborate Gothic canopies.

The importance of Pugin in establishing a revival of authentic Gothic design and technique cannot be exaggerated. It was matched by a parallel development of the craft's raw material, the glass itself, in a largely successful effort to produce coloured pot-metal glass of similar character to that of the Middle Ages. The period 1850-60 saw

Figs. 19 and 20. *These two windows by A W N Pugin, earliest examples of fully medievalist Victorian glass in Oxford, were given to the church by the comic actor George Bartley as memorials to two of his children, depicted as kneeling figures in the manner of medieval donors. The earlier window (19) shows Thomas Bartley, a student of Exeter College, with his academic gown and 'mortar-board' while the later window (20) depicts his sister Sophia with her ringlets, shawl and crinoline. As images of family piety they reveal the profound way in which the Victorians identified with the spirituality as well as the art of their medieval ancestors. (University Church of St Mary the Virgin, windows 7 and 9)*

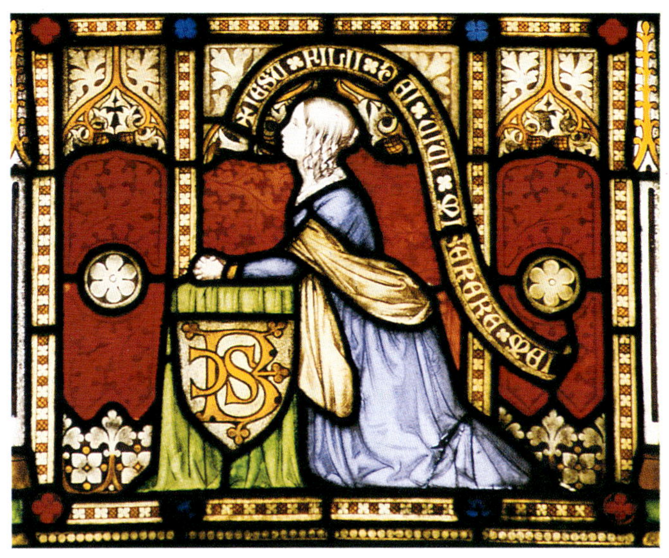

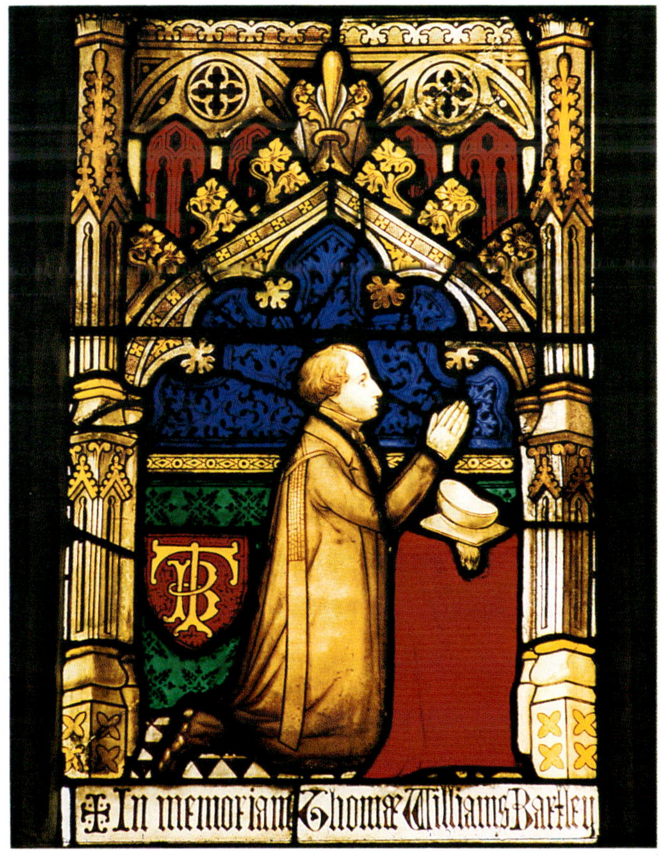
In memoriam Thomæ Williams Bartley

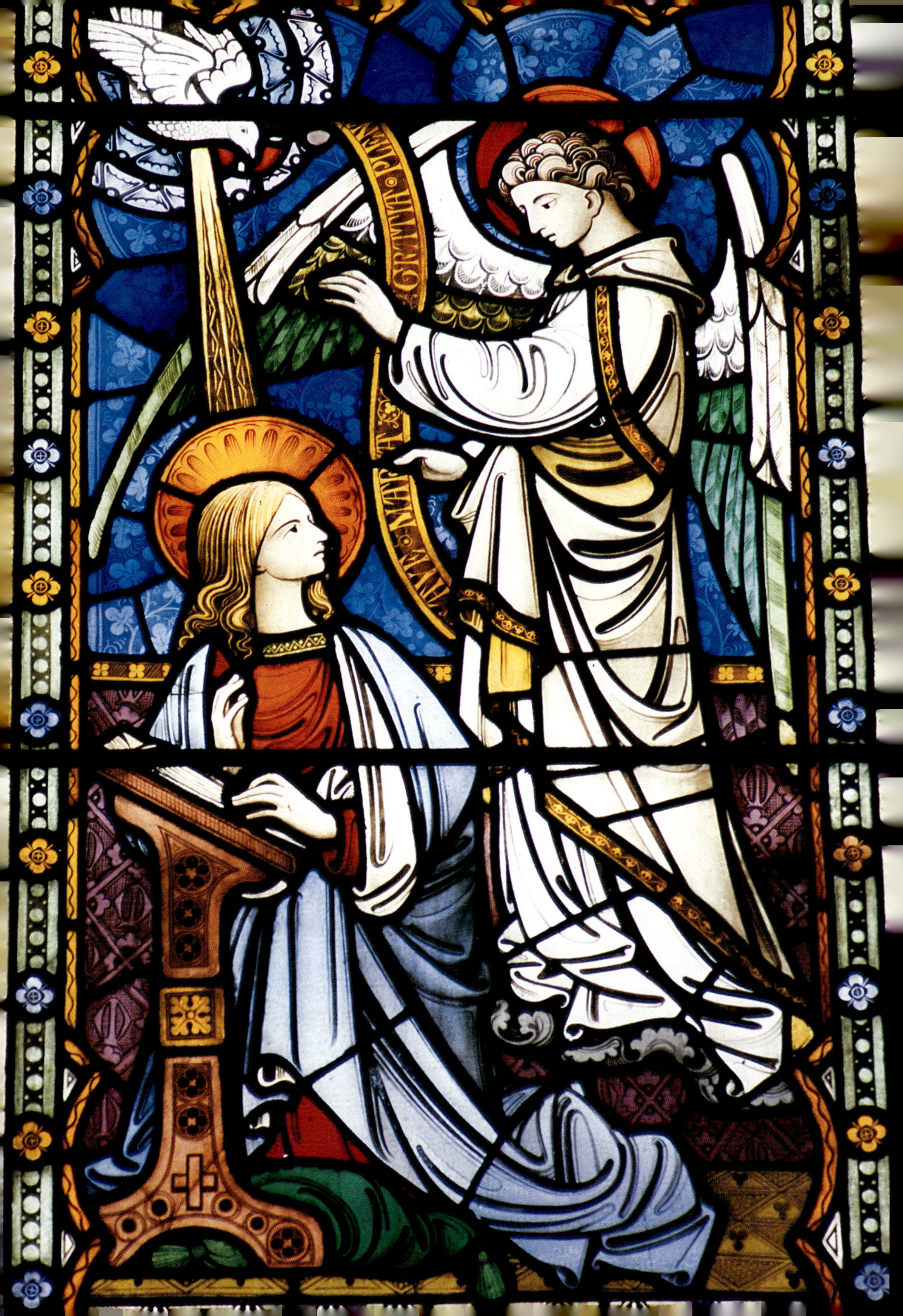
AVE · MARIA
GRATIA

a huge expansion in the number of stained glass studios throughout the country. One of the most prolific was that of William Wailes of Newcastle, who for a time collaborated with Pugin. The latter's influence can be seen in Wailes' work in the church of St Mary Magdalen and in Brasenose College chapel. Wailes' studio is typical of the large-scale stained glass manufacturers, known to later critics as 'The Trade', who were to dominate English stained glass until the turn of the century.

This early period in the life of the large firms witnessed a number of important collaborations between architect and stained glass studio, partnerships which, through the vision and foresight of such architects of stature as Sir George Gilbert Scott and William Butterfield, produced windows that rose above the potentially detrimental effects of industrial mass production. In their work for Scott in Exeter College chapel, Clayton & Bell produced an excellent series of windows which harmonize perfectly with the architecture of the building. In the form of tall narrow lancets, the Exeter windows really do create a similar atmosphere to the great Sainte Chapelle in Paris, which Scott took as the model for his design. The use of Types and Antitypes — analogous incidents from the Old and New Testaments — for the subject matter further enhances the medieval effect.

At Keble College, Alexander Gibbs' chapel windows were conceived as an integral part of the overall polychrome decoration, which included mosaic and tiling. The whole scheme was executed under the strict supervision of architect William Butterfield, a man as rigorous in his views on stained glass as Pugin himself. The college was intended to embody the ideals of the Oxford Movement and it was therefore natural that the chapel should be decorated in a way which emphasized the religious ideas of Anglo-Catholicism. Windows depicting the Evangelists are faced by ones containing those prophets most closely associated with the foretelling of the Incarnation, while

Fig. 21. The Annunciation, from one of the apse windows in the chapel of Exeter College, shows Clayton & Bell's skill as glass-painters, particularly in the almost calligraphic drawing of the drapery folds and the delicate pattern-work in the background. Although deliberately medievalist in design, the rich colouring of the glass also suggests the influence of contemporary Pre-Raphaelite painting. Significantly, J R Clayton, the principal designer of the apse windows at Exeter, was an associate of Rossetti and his circle. (Exeter College Chapel, window 15)

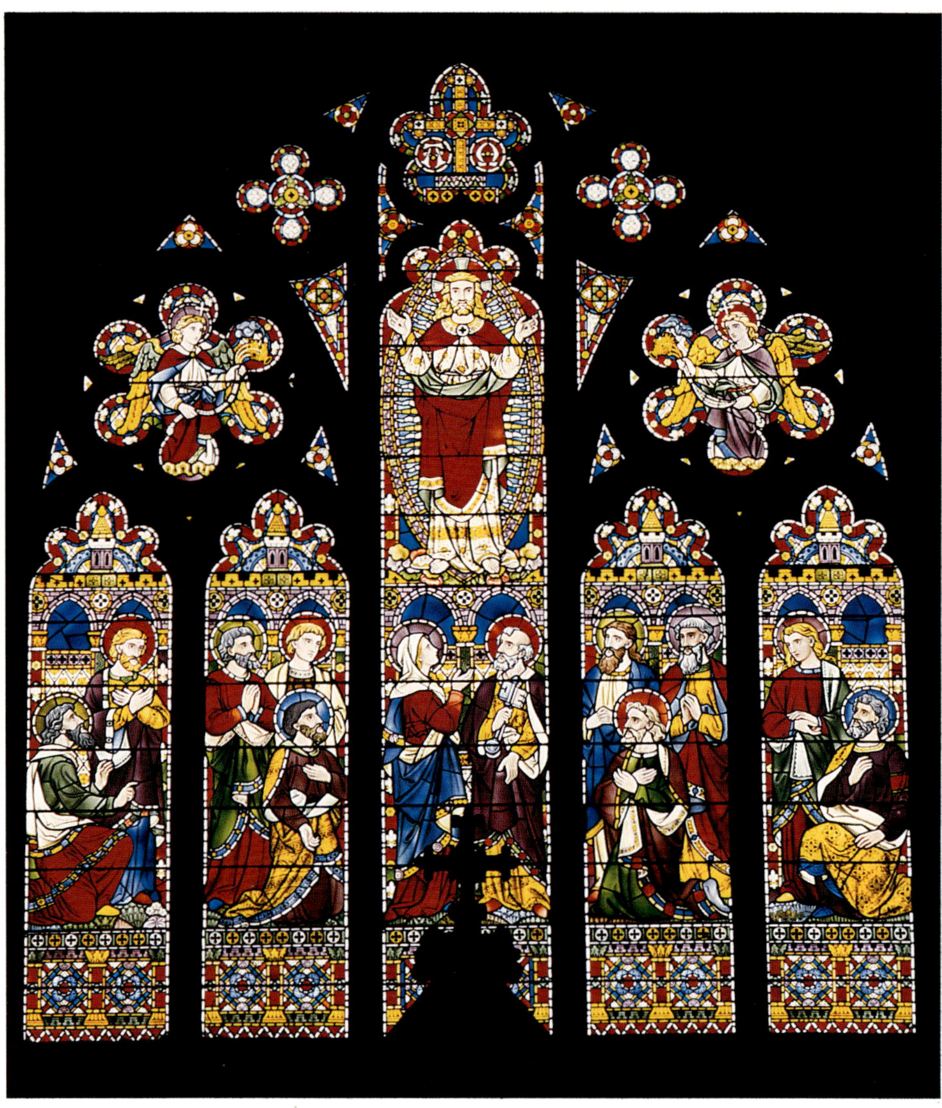

Fig. 22. *Alex Gibbs' windows at Keble were all executed under the close supervision of the architect William Butterfield, who used the glass as a richly luminous element within his overall scheme of decoration. In the east window the severely geometric patterns and boldly delineated figures create the effect of an illuminated mosaic, repeating some of the motifs used in the mural decoration and altar furnishings beneath. (Keble College Chapel, window 1)*

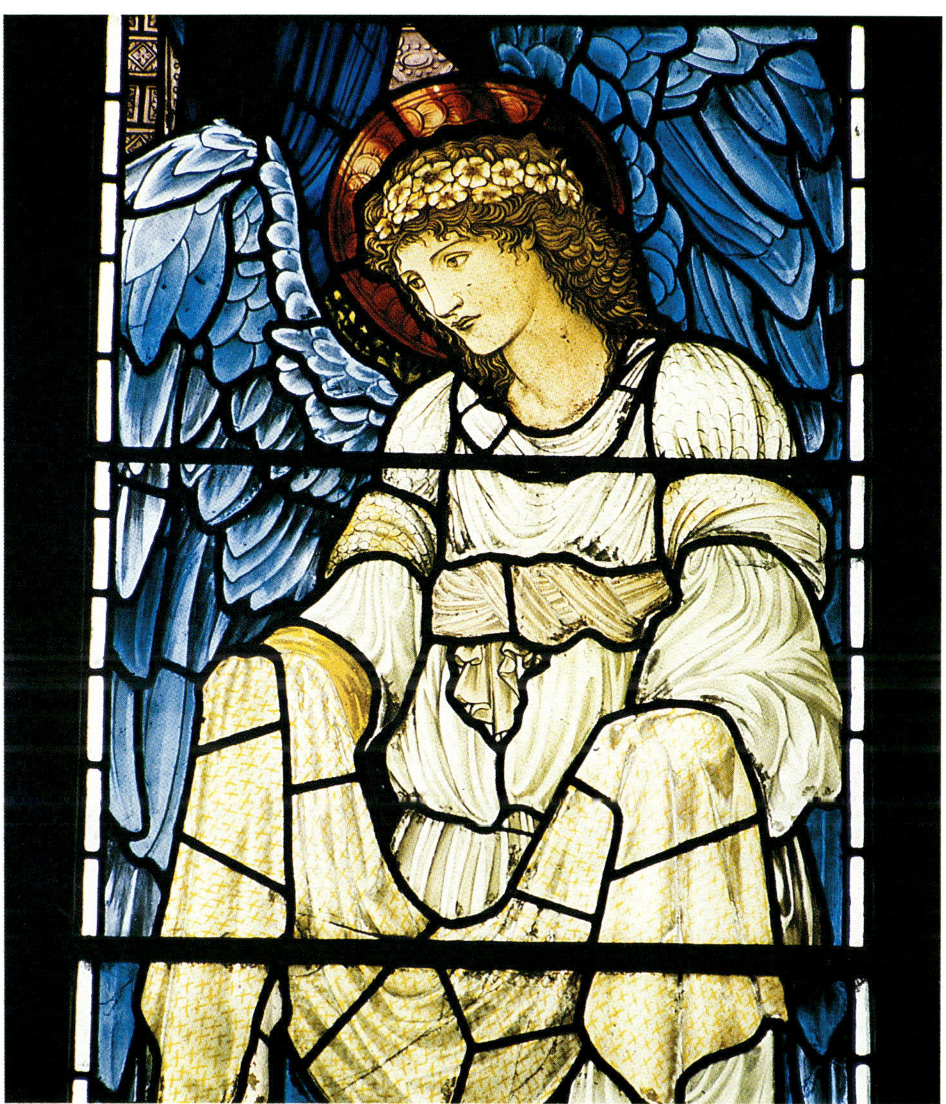

Fig. 23. Detail from the St Catherine window, designed by Burne-Jones and made by Morris, Marshall, Faulkner & Co, commemorates Edith Liddell, sister of Alice (immortalized in the books of Lewis Carroll). A masterpiece of Burne-Jones' mature style, it shows his admiration for the Italian Renaissance painters of the 15th century. The influence of Botticelli is particularly evident in this graceful Angel with her beautifully drawn features and elaborate drapery. (Christ Church Cathedral, window 4)

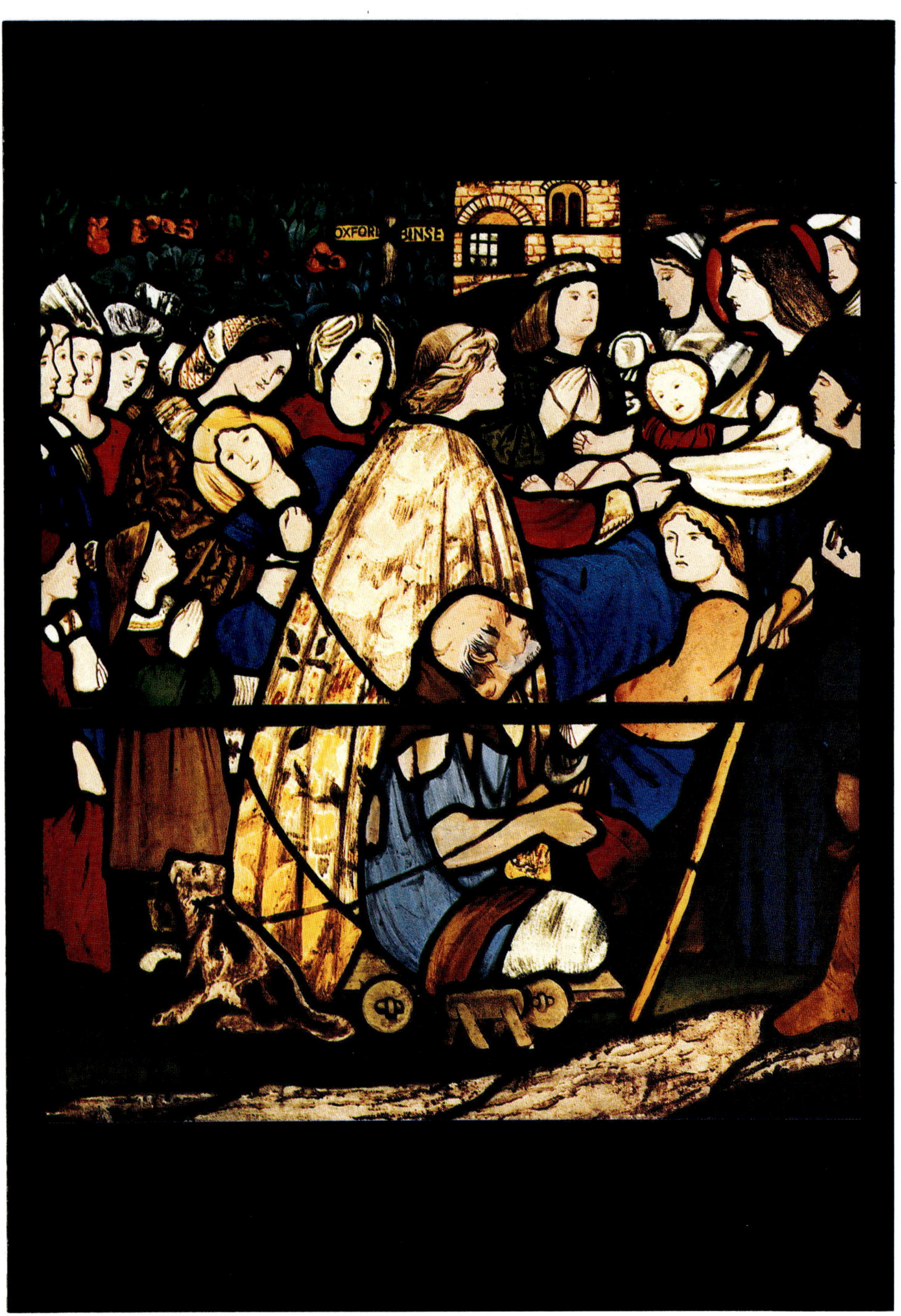
OXFORD
BINSE

the window above the altar, with Christ and the Apostles, is flanked by a series showing the Doctors of the Church, whose writings had inspired Keble and his colleagues in the Oxford Movement.

Edward Burne-Jones and William Morris

Pugin's approach to the Gothic style, often less imaginatively interpreted, remained influential in many firms well into the 1870s. This pre-eminence was to be challenged, however, by the work of Edward Burne-Jones, a former undergraduate of Exeter College. His St Frideswide window of 1859 in Christ Church Cathedral, commissioned on the instructions of the architect Benjamin Woodward, evoked the spirit of medieval glass without any direct imitations of its forms. The window is one of the masterpieces of Victorian stained glass, glowing with a kaleidoscopic range of colours and crammed with narrative scenes reminiscent of Pre-Raphaelite wood engravings. The window tells the story of Oxford's patron saint, from her upbringing by Saints Cecilia and Catherine to her death in the nunnery, which she founded in the city. The most colourful and dramatic scenes are those in which she is shown fleeing the unwelcome attentions of her suitor, the King of Mercia, who is depicted in late-medieval costume with a colourful retinue of courtiers and knights. Despite the medieval setting, however, Burne-Jones' figures are not drawn in the stylized Gothic idiom favoured by Pugin and his followers; they are, in pose and expression, as naturalistically conceived as the characters in a Pre-Raphaelite painting, with the same sense of dramatic intensity. This is especially evident in the scenes of St Frideswide hiding in the pigsty as the King's soldiers go perilously near by, and of the King struck blind in retribution for his pursuit of the saint.

In 1861, Burne-Jones and his friend, fellow Exeter student William Morris, joined the painter Dante Gabriel Rossetti, the

Fig. 24. Detail from Burne-Jones' St Frideswide window, one of his earliest works in stained glass, pre-dating his partnership with William Morris. Its crowded narrative scenes and sparkling colours typify the Pre-Raphaelites' imaginative brand of medievalism. (Christ Church Cathedral, window 28)

architect Philip Webb (who was born and trained in Oxford) and others to form the firm of Morris, Marshall, Faulkner & Co (later simply Morris & Co). The partners proclaimed their conviction that a return to the medieval ideals of craftsmanship would rescue the applied arts from commercialism and industrialization. From the outset, stained glass was one of the firm's most important productions. Their earliest Oxford window, for the chapel of St Edmund Hall (1864), was a collaborative work in the best medieval tradition, incorporating designs by three of the partners, Burne-Jones, Morris and Webb. To progressive designers frustrated by the limitations of neo-Gothic, its subtle, almost muted, colouring and naturalistic figure-style suggested an alternative to strict historicism. To see how radically Morris & Co were departing from the orthodoxy of mid-Victorian stained glass design, one need only compare their altar window at St Edmund Hall chapel with the contemporary Clayton & Bell windows in the same chapel which, in colouring and style, are indebted to Pugin.

One of the finest Victorian interiors to show the impact of this new approach is to be found at Worcester College, where the chapel was refurbished by the architect William Burges from 1864 to 1865. Burges chose a classical style for the scheme of decoration, which included a painted frieze and seven stained glass windows by Henry Holiday, a painter strongly influenced by the example of Morris & Co. The success of this remarkable ensemble owes much to the impression created by Holiday's wholly un-medieval windows with their superbly-drawn figures and their palette of dark reds, browns, blues and golds with large areas of white or pale tinted glass, a most unusual combination for its time. The window over the altar, a Crucifixion with the Virgin and St John, displays a cool solemnity, while the tortured emotionalism of some medievalist versions of this subject is replaced by a controlled intensity. Holiday drew his figures

Fig. 25. A serene classicism marks Henry Holiday's windows at Worcester College. In this Crucifixion scene the solemn drama is emphasized by the absence of patterned borders and by the austere background scenery. Few Victorian windows make such a direct impact on the spectator. (Worcester College Chapel, window 1)

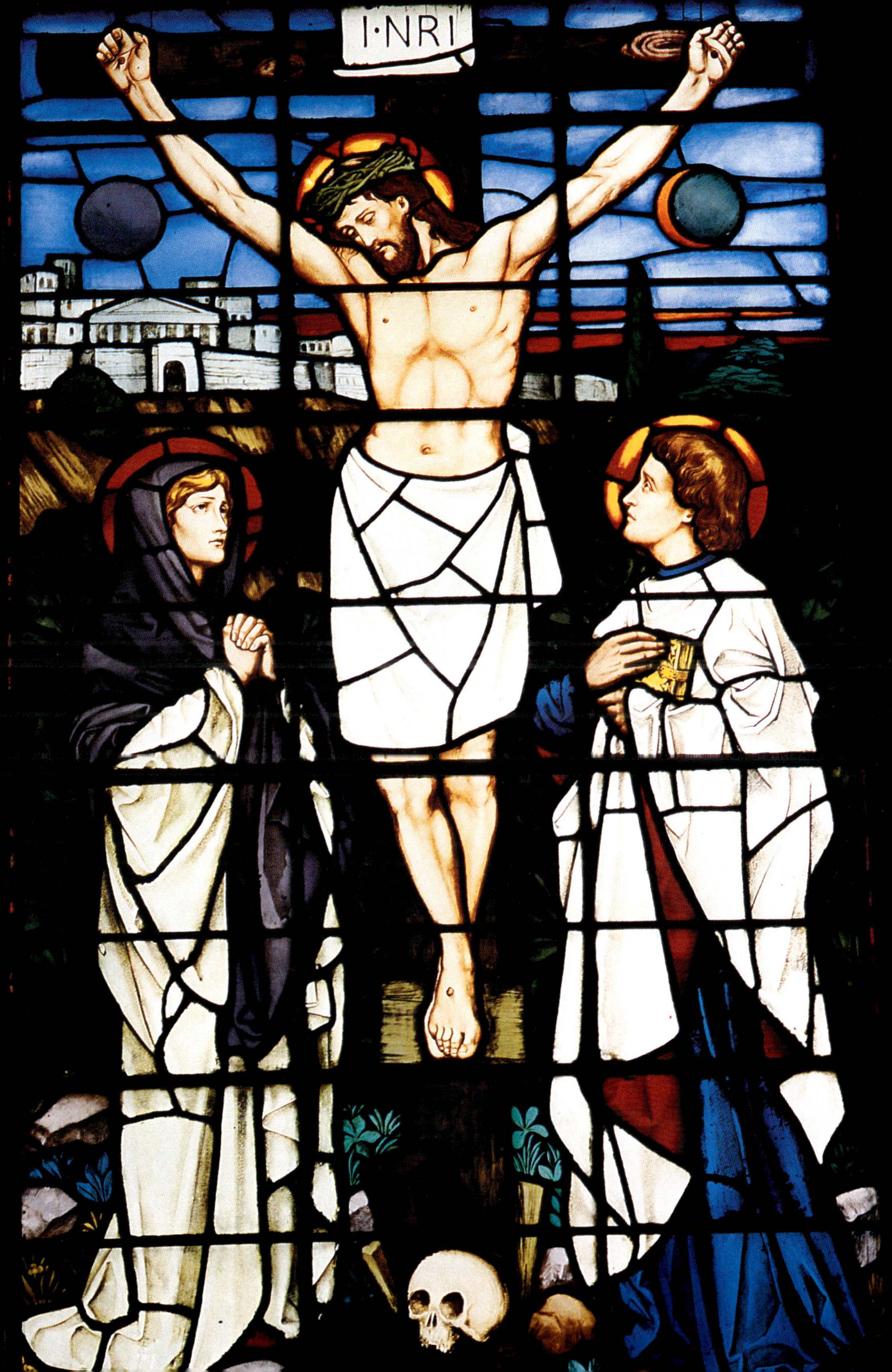
I·NRI

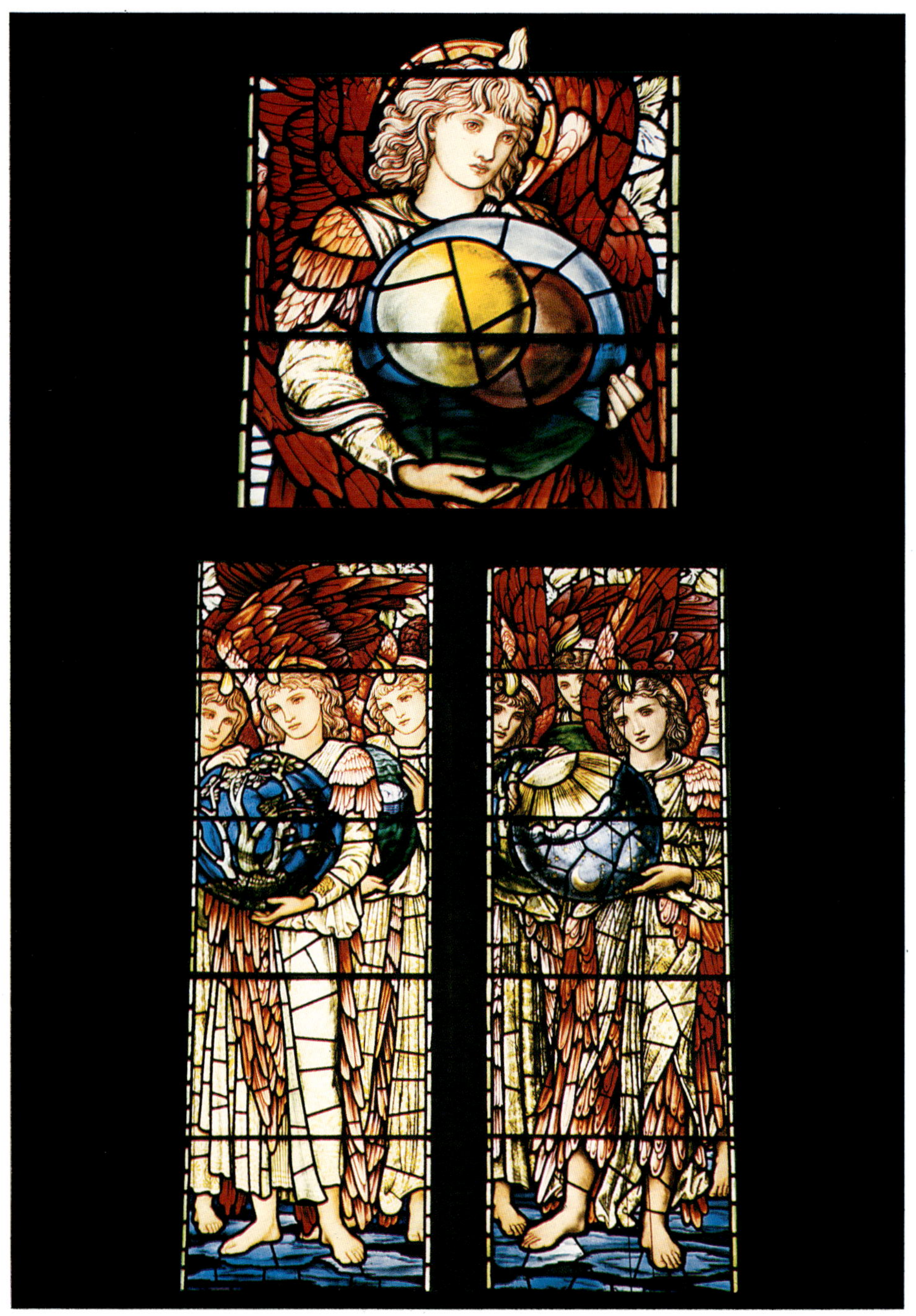

from life, unlike many of his contemporaries, and in the simple rectangular openings of the college was able to dispense with distracting Gothic ornamentation. A comparison of the Worcester windows with those at Exeter reveals not only how widely stained glass styles had diverged by the 1860s, but also the wide diversity of Victorian religious sensibilities.

The later development of Morris & Co's stained glass is essentially the story of Burne-Jones' stylistic evolution as a designer. The four windows which he designed for Christ Church Cathedral in the 1870s are probably the best known post-medieval glass in Oxford. One scarcely recognizes the creator of the St Frideswide window in these pallid, graceful, Italianate works. The figures have a sculptural quality, enhanced by their almost monochrome colouring, contrasted with deeper backgrounds of foliage or damask pattern designed by Morris in burgundy, prussian blue or dark green. The loveliest of these windows, both in its design and execution, depicts St Catherine with attendant angels. Three incidents from her life fill predella panels below. The face of St Catherine herself is a likeness of Edith Liddell, whom the window commemorates; she was the sister of Alice Liddell, immortalized in the books and photographs of the Revd C L Dodgson, better known as Lewis Carroll. It was perhaps from one of Dodgson's photographs that Burne-Jones drew St Catherine's face.

Burne-Jones' other major Oxford work for Morris & Co is to be found in Manchester College chapel, which contains a complete scheme of windows made between 1893 and 1899. They are more richly coloured than the earlier Christ Church Cathedral windows, particularly the three depicting the Angels of Creation — based on a series of paintings by Burne-Jones — who each hold a sphere containing a scene from the Genesis story. Ruby and 'gold-pink' glass is contrasted with deep blues in the central panels of each light, while above and below the figures are sinuous designs of pale green foliage.

Figs. 26 and 27. The Six Days of Creation are represented by Angels holding symbolic spheres (each depicting a stage in the Genesis story) in these windows designed by Burne-Jones and made by Morris & Co. The subject was adapted from a series of pictures which Burne-Jones painted in the 1870s. The inter-weaving foliage patterns are much like those in Morris's wallpapers and textiles. (Manchester College Chapel, windows 4 and 5)

The best work of Burne-Jones and Henry Holiday showed their contemporaries that stained glass could be a genuinely modern and innovative art-form, and that designers could seek inspiration from all the great traditions of art, not just from the Gothic. In architecture, a similar eclecticism was challenging the stylistic supremacy of Gothic: the champion of the new style in Oxford was Thomas Graham Jackson, whose flamboyant buildings (such as the Examination Schools of 1876-82) display a picturesque mixture of English Renaissance and later details. In the 1880s and 1890s Jackson refurbished many of the college chapels and in two of these, Brasenose and Oriel, there is excellent glass by a former assistant of both Burne-Jones and Holiday — Harry Ellis Wooldridge. The Brasenose chapel window has finely-drawn figures derived from Italian painting of the 15th century; particularly striking is the figure of St Michael in his ornate Florentine armour — a figure that could almost have stepped out of a Botticelli altar-piece. Wooldridge also drew upon Renaissance models for his six windows in Oriel chapel; indeed, each of the Oriel windows has an identical Annunciation scene, based on a Quattrocento painting, in the tracery light. The window over the altar is an exuberantly Italianate Adoration of the Magi and Shepherds with finely-drawn figures and an unusual range of colours closer to the palette of an easel painter than that of the traditional stained glass artist. The window is none the less executed in the traditional technique, making an interesting contrast with Peckitt's painterly window of 1767, executed in enamel colours. Wooldridge's other windows in Oriel chapel depict founders and benefactors of the college, and saints and prophets, the latter framed by Italianate architectural borders and canopies, creating the effect of sculpture within niches. Wooldridge, whose work deserves to be better known, had a distinguished Oxford career after retiring as a stained glass designer: he succeeded John Ruskin as Slade Professor of Art.

Fig. 28. In this Nativity scene, the Magi and Shepherds are conceived in the manner of a Renaissance altar-piece. The quality of the glass-painting, for example in the faces and patterned drapery, reveals the skills of Powell's craftsmen who translated Wooldridge's design into glass. (Oriel College Chapel, window 1)

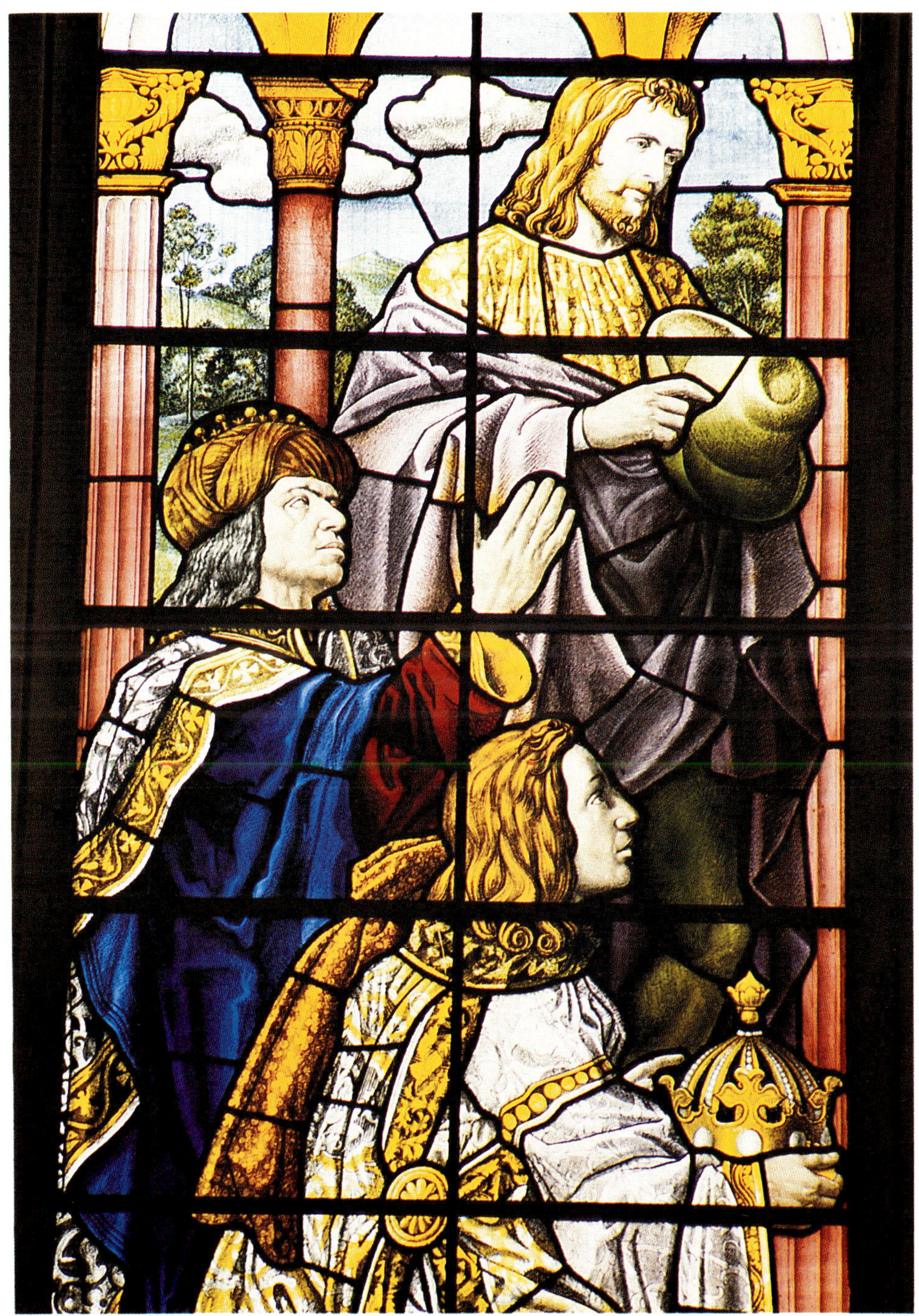

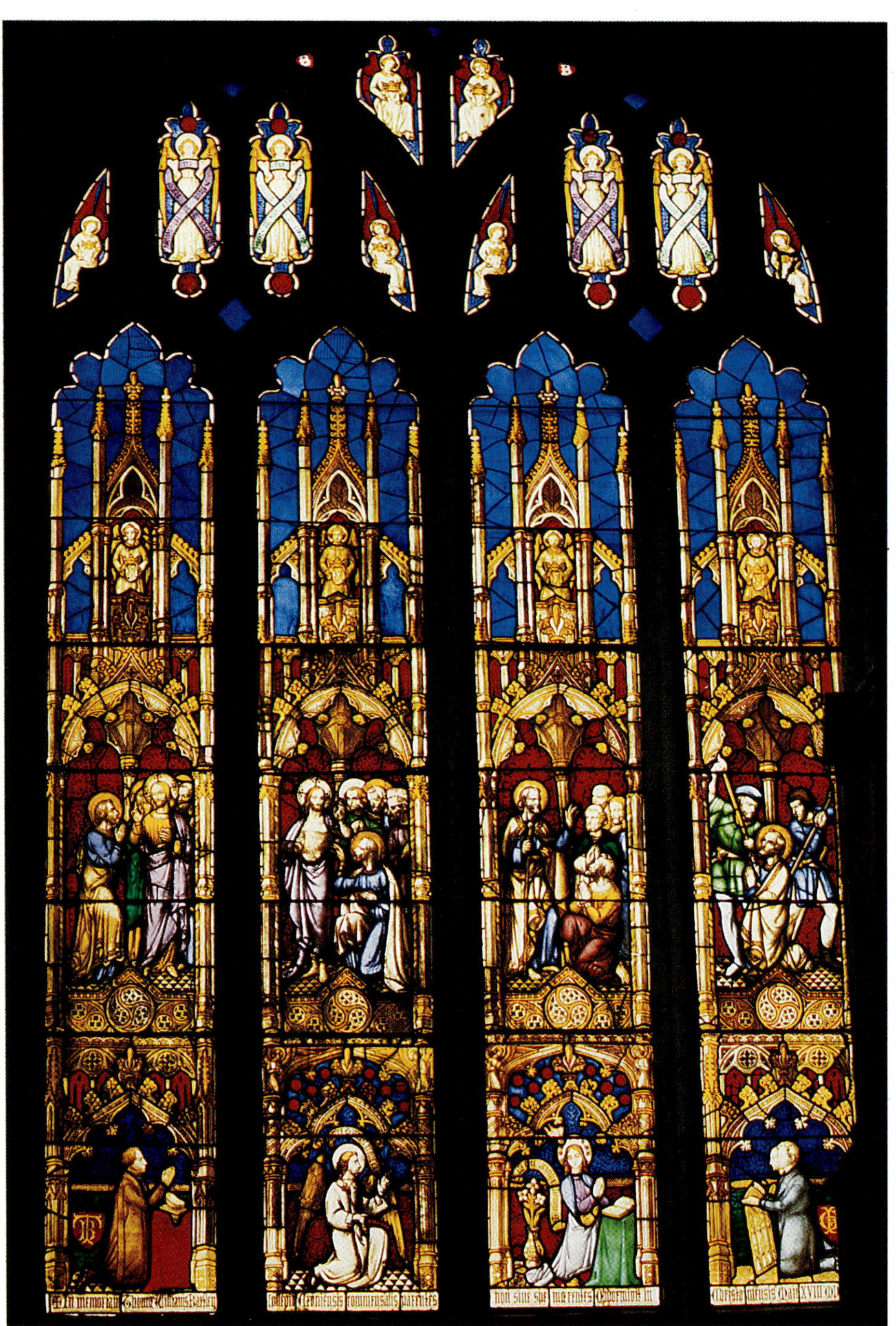

While 'progressive' designers experimented with style, at the same time remaining faithful to medieval techniques of craftsmanship, other designers stayed firmly within the neo-Gothic tradition. It was the robust Gothic style of the 13th and 14th centuries that had inspired Pugin and his followers, but it was to the art of the 15th and early 16th centuries in England and the Low Countries that the later Victorians looked for a more delicate style of stained glass. In Oxford the surviving medieval glass in the chapels of New College and All Souls was an obvious source of ideas. This is particularly evident in the work of Clayton & Bell (who restored the All Souls windows in the 1870s) where the rich primary colours and bold designs of their Exeter College chapel windows of the 1860s give way to a paler colour scheme with much use of architectural canopy-work in white glass, as in the side windows of All Souls and St John's.

The leading figure in this more conservative school was Charles Eamer Kempe, some of whose best work is in the chapel of his old college, Pembroke, which he completely refurbished in the 1880s. The ornate Pembroke windows were based upon 16th-century Flemish glass, but perhaps more typical of Kempe's very prolific output are the windows in Jesus College chapel and the large west window in the church of St Mary the Virgin (1891). In the latter, a host of angels, prophets and patriarchs is bedecked in pearled and jewelled late-Gothic vestments and framed in curling foliage. This is the epitome of Anglo Catholic artistic taste, the visual counterpart of the religious ritualism favoured by later members of the Oxford Movement. Kempe's work was widely copied and formed the basis of a style which continued well into the present century, represented at its best by Ninian Comper's large choir window (*c.* 1913) in the chapel of Pusey House.

Fig. 29. This lovely window, designed by a A W N Pugin in 1843, depicts scenes from the Life of St Thomas. The kneeling figure, in the bottom left-hand corner, is Thomas Bartley who appears as a detail in Fig. 19. (University Church of St Mary the Virgin, window 7)

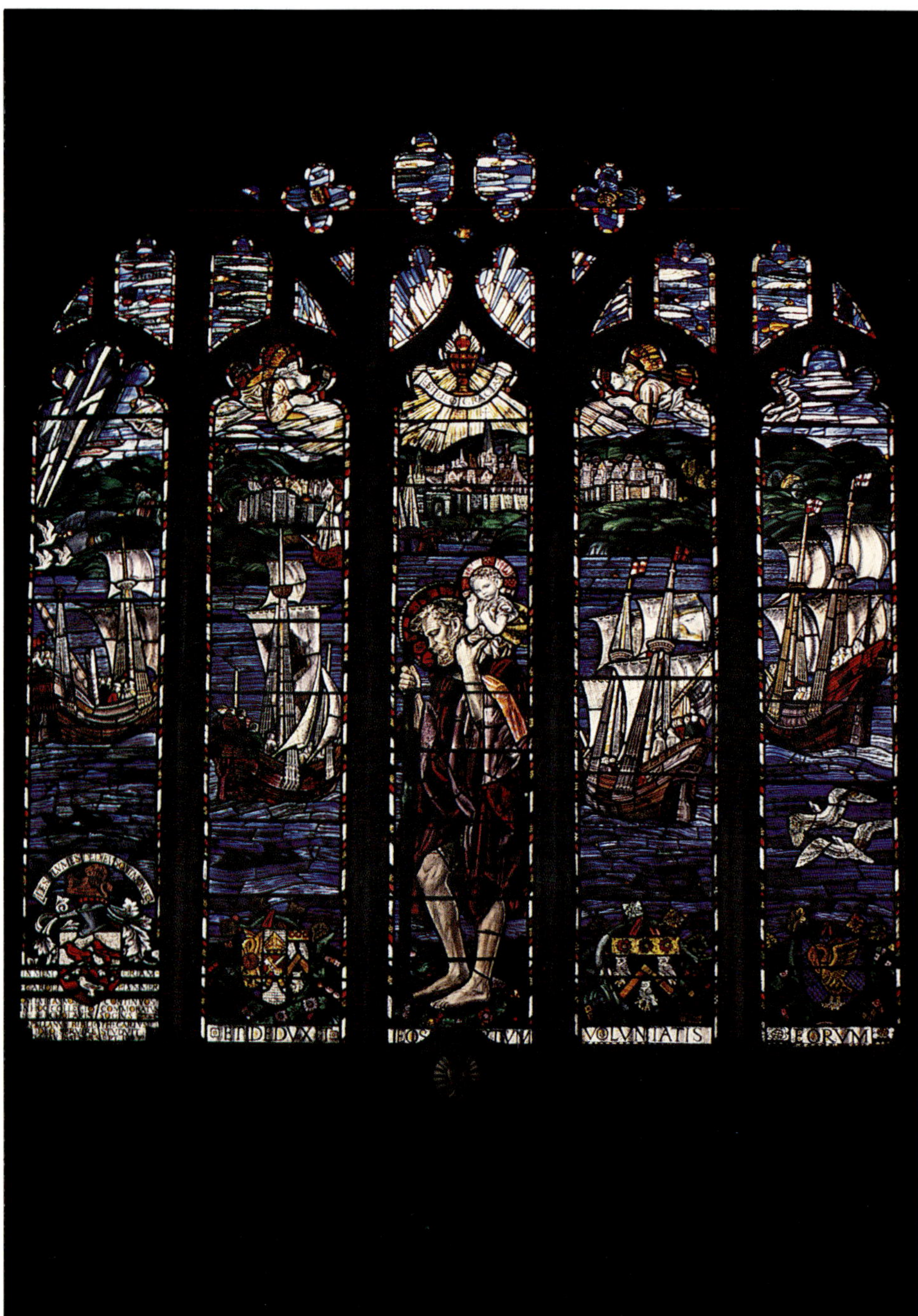
ET DEDVX
EOS
VOLVNTATIS
EORVM

TWENTIETH-CENTURY EXPERIMENTATION

The success of the Victorian stained glass revival and the consequent growth of a sizeable industry inevitably led to commercialized mass production methods, entailing a sacrifice of artistic quality and traditional craft values. A reaction against this commercialism in the applied arts was the impetus behind the Arts and Crafts Movement at the turn of the century, whose leading representative in stained glass was Christopher Whall. Although there are no examples of Whall's work in Oxford — his design for Hertford College chapel (*c.* 1920) was never carried out — windows designed and made by him can be found at Somerton and Burford in the county, and there is an accomplished window by one of his pupils, Henry Payne, in Corpus Christi chapel (1931). It was designed, painted and made entirely in his own studio-workshop and has many of the hallmarks of the Arts and Crafts style: excellent draughtsmanship, a highly original treatment of the subject matter (St Christopher with the Christ Child with a seascape), and richly glowing colours with a 'stippled' glass-painting technique which controls and manipulates the light within each piece of glass.

Experimentation with craft techniques and a gradual abandonment of historicism are the chief characteristics of the 20th-century approach to stained glass. Oxford's churches and chapels are typical of others throughout Britain in having an extensive heritage of Victorian glazing which has limited the opportunities for modern designers and craftsmen. The windows at St John's College chapel by Ervin Bossanyi (1944) and at Nuffield, designed by John Piper and executed by Patrick Reyntiens (1961), are rare examples of a modern idiom in

Fig. 30. A superbly drawn figure of St Christopher with the Christ Child is the central subject of the only stained glass window in Corpus Christi College Chapel. It was designed and made by Henry Payne, who worked in the Arts and Crafts tradition pioneered by Christopher Whall at the turn of the century. Apart from its impressive craftsmanship, the window illustrates the very original approach to subject matter which is typical of Arts and Crafts designers. The City itelf is depicted in great detail and bears some resemblance to medieval views of Oxford. (Corpus Christi College Chapel, window 1)

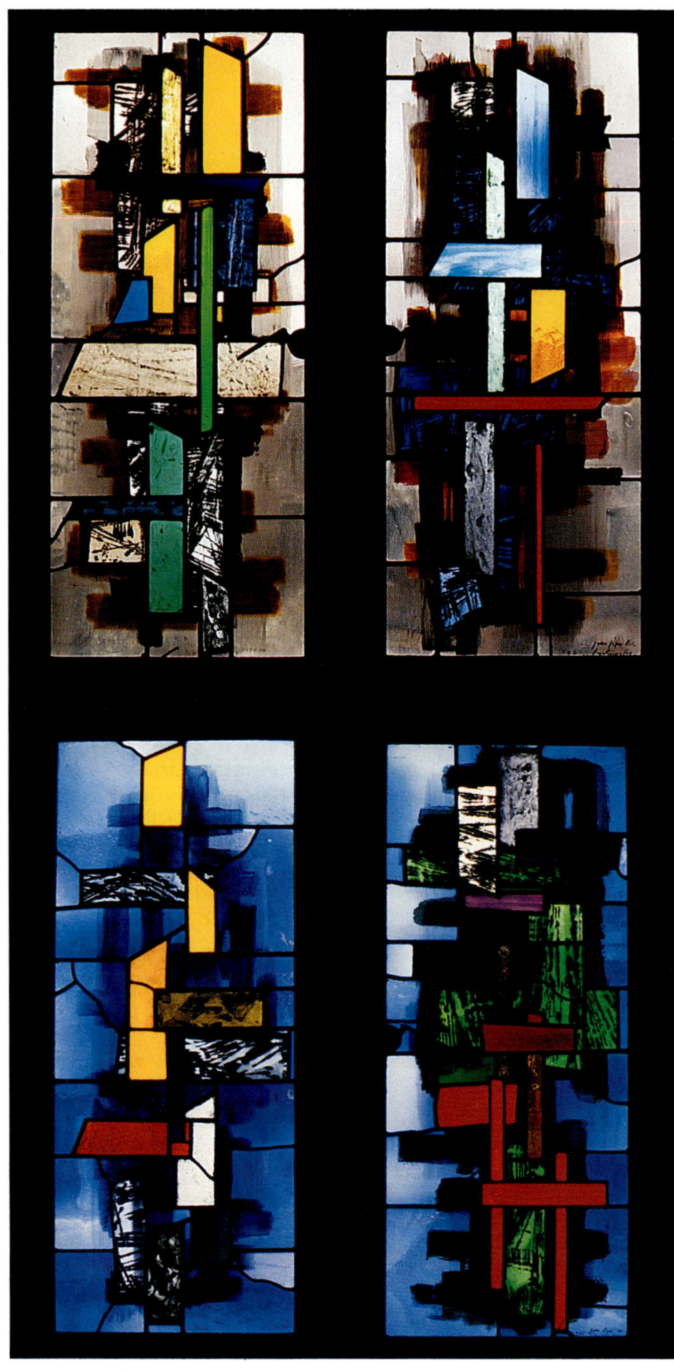

stained glass, in both cases revealing the diverse forms of Expressionism. Bossanyi's glass at St John's was not designed for the building but is certainly a colourful and attractive addition to the chapel. The artist, a Hungarian who had worked in Germany before coming to England in the 1930s, combines a powerfully emotional style with consummate craftsmanship; his figures are dramatically posed both in relation to each other and within the framework of the window and are drawn in a graphic, linear manner — a modernist reinterpretation of the style of early medieval glass. In contrast, the abstract symbolism of the Piper/Reyntiens windows confronts the spectator with something closer to the bare essentials of stained glass — light and colour, devoid of all but the vaguest forms, used as expressive vehicles in themselves. Although now over twenty-five years old, the Nuffield windows are still the most radically modern glass to be seen in Oxford. In his more recent work in Christ Church Hall (1983), Patrick Reyntiens has used a consciously neo-Victorian style, reworking an artistic tradition that has contributed so much to Oxford's heritage of stained glass.

Thus, the history of stained glass in the city of Oxford has come almost full circle. The city now offers a collection of windows of a variety and quality almost unparalleled in England. Only York can rival Oxford for the title 'city of stained glass', and even York cannot match Oxford for the wealth of post-medieval windows. Having suffered the vagaries of the Reformation, Oxford has been the one place in England where the Laudian Revival of the 17th century and the Gothic Revival of the 19th century have done much to re-create the rich stained glass heritage that the medieval visitor would have expected to find.

Figs. 31 and 32. Light, colour and abstract form are the expressive medium which John Piper and Patrick Reyntiens used for their windows at Nuffield College, made in 1965–6. Although the style is uncompromisingly modern, the techniques used are essentially the same as those of the Middle Ages, testifying to the infinite capacity of the craft to inspire artists of periods and outlooks. (Nuffield College Chapel, windows 2 and 5)

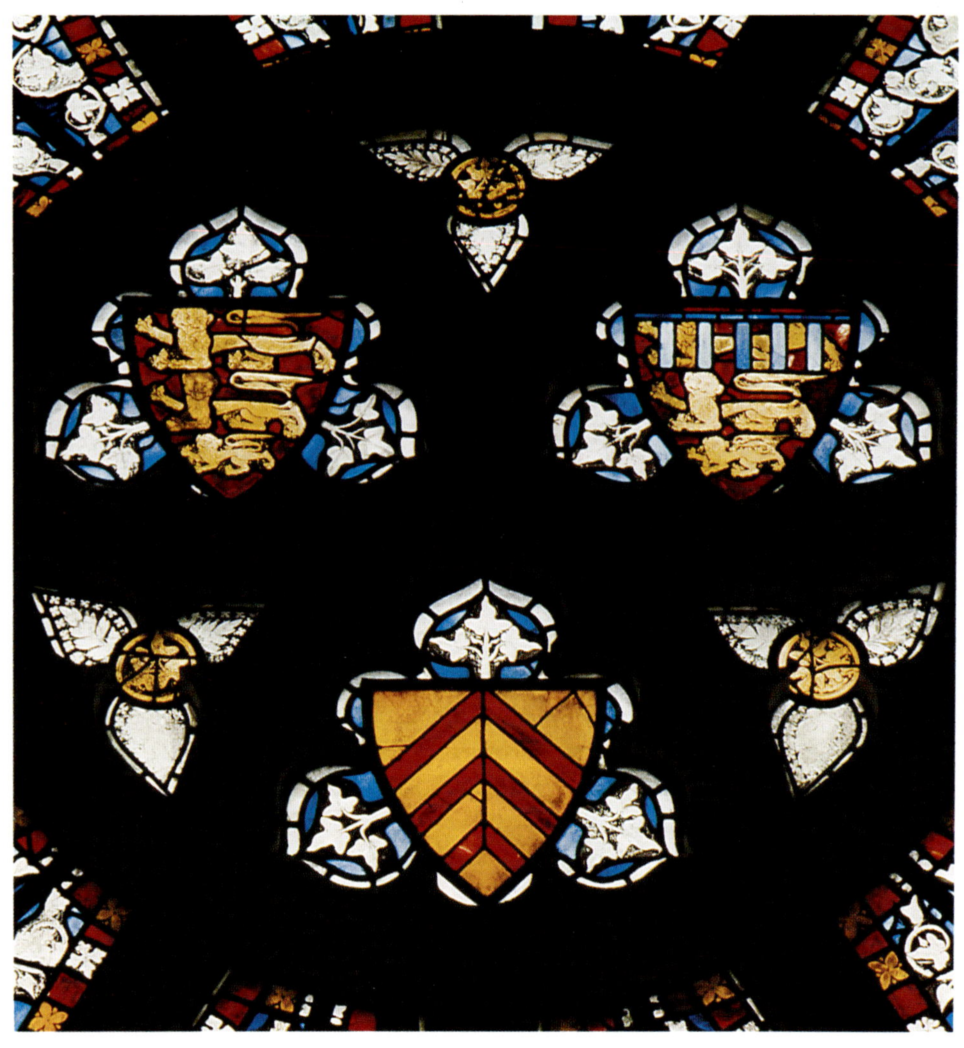

***Fig. 33**. Detail from the east window, Merton College Chapel, late 13th century. (Merton College Chapel, window 1)*

TABLE OF STAINED GLASS IN OXFORD CHAPELS AND CHURCHES OVER THE CENTURIES

Colleges	*13C*	*14C*	*15C*	*16C*	*17C*	*18C*	*19C*	*20C*
ALL SOULS			★				★	
BALLIOL			★	★	★			
BRASENOSE						★	★	
CHRIST CHURCH		★	★	★	★		★	★
CORPUS CHRISTI								★
EXETER							★	
JESUS							★	
KEBLE							★	
LINCOLN					★			
MAGDALEN					★		★	
MANCHESTER							★	
MERTON	★	★	★					
NEW COLLEGE		★				★	★	
NUFFIELD								★
ORIEL				★			★	
PEMBROKE							★	
PUSEY HOUSE								★
QUEEN'S				★	★	★		
ST EDMUND HALL							★	
ST JOHN'S							★	★
ST PETER'S							★	★
TRINITY							★	
UNIVERSITY					★		★	
WADHAM				★	★		★	
WORCESTER							★	
Churches								
ST EBBE			★				★	
ST MARY THE VIRGIN							★	★
ST MARY MAGDALEN							★	
ST MICHAEL	★		★					★

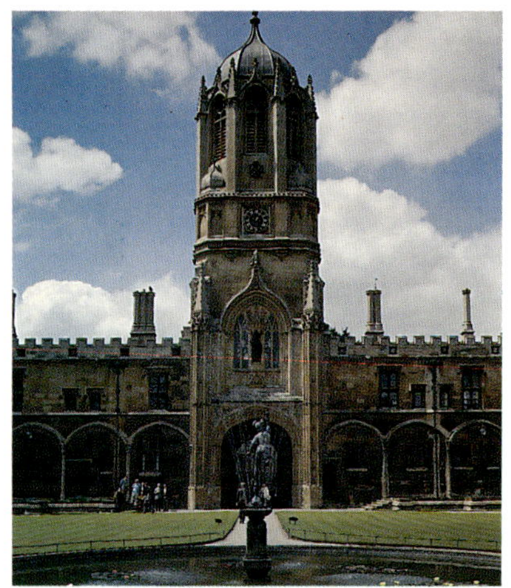

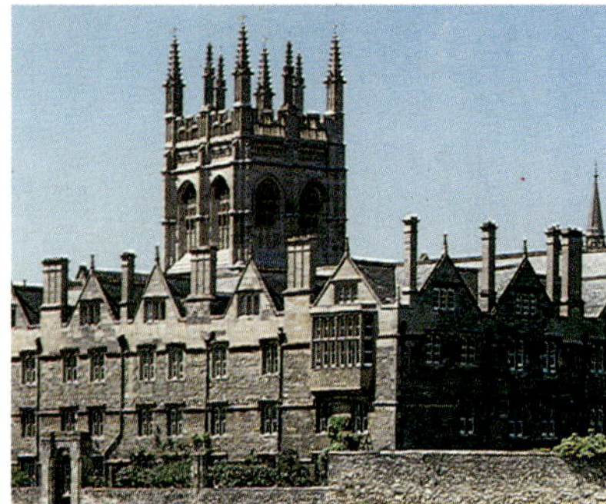

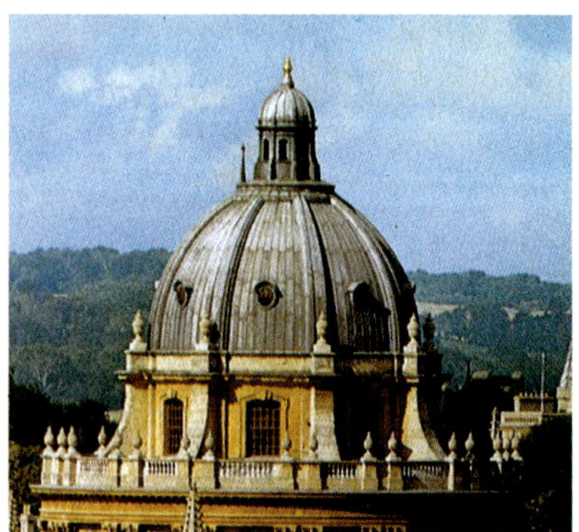

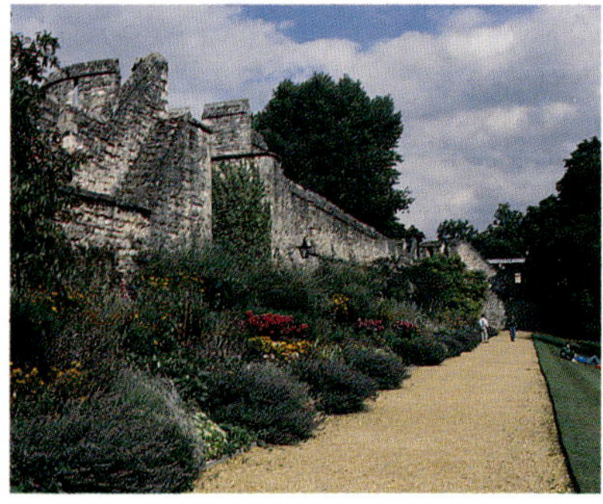

HIGHLIGHTS: A GUIDED WALK

A splendid way to see some of the best stained glass in Oxford, is by following the route of this short walk (see map opposite), beginning with Christ Church in St Aldate's. ***Christ Church (1)*** The Cathedral contains one of the largest and most varied collections of stained glass (early 14th-century Becket window; Jonah before Ninevah by Abraham van Linge, 1630s; Edward Burne-Jones' St Frideswide window of 1859). The Great Hall contains Reyntiens' Alice in Wonderland windows of 1983. ***Corpus Christi College (2)*** has the only Oxford window in the Arts and Crafts tradition, St Christopher and the Christ Child. ***Merton College (3)*** purports to be Oxford's oldest college; its late 13th-century chapel windows, given by Master Henry de Mamesfeld, are some of the most important in England, ***University College Chapel (4)*** displays probably the finest works by Abraham van Linge (1641), including Adam and Eve, and Jonah and a particularly toothy whale. ***All Souls College Antechapel (5)*** retains its mid-15th-century glass by the workshop of John Glasier, depicting the Apostles and a series of female saints dressed in the height of fashion. ***The Church of St Mary the Virgin (6)*** is visible for its spire that jostles with the Radcliffe Camera for mastery of the skyline. It contains the earliest Gothic Revival window in the city, A W N Pugin's window of 1843, which reinstated the use of donor figures. ***Lincoln College (7)*** is one of the few medieval colleges substantially unchanged by the passing of time, with chapel windows (1629–31) by Abraham van Linge; compare this Jonah and the Whale with the one at University College. ***Exeter College Chapel (8)*** is one of Sir Gilbert Scott's most impressive designs and certainly his finest church interior. Old and New Testament Windows by Clayton & Bell, 1859–90. ***New College (9)*** offers medieval cloisters, a lovely garden and a splendid view of the city walls — in addition to a magnificent chapel containing striking prophets and saints by Thomas Glasier (1380–6), stately saints and royal figures by William Price (1735–40) and William Peckitt (1765 and 1774), and Sir Joshua Reynolds' controversial Virtues of 1775–85. ***Manchester College (10)*** is a relative late-comer to the University, but the only one to boast a complete scheme of windows by Morris & Co (1895–9). Particularly striking are the Angels of the Creation, ***Wadham College (11)*** is a perfect expression of early 17th-century taste, hardly altered since its completion in 1613. Bernard van Linge's only work in Oxford. Should you be making your way back to the railway station, or have some time left, try to visit the charming ***Worcester College*** with its beautiful gardens, large lake and mature trees. The splendid chapel contains a complete decorative scheme (1864-5) by William Burges and Henry Holiday, presided over by a graceful Crucifixion above the altar.

(a) Christ Church *(c) Radcliffe Camera*

(b) Merton College *(d) New College Gardens*

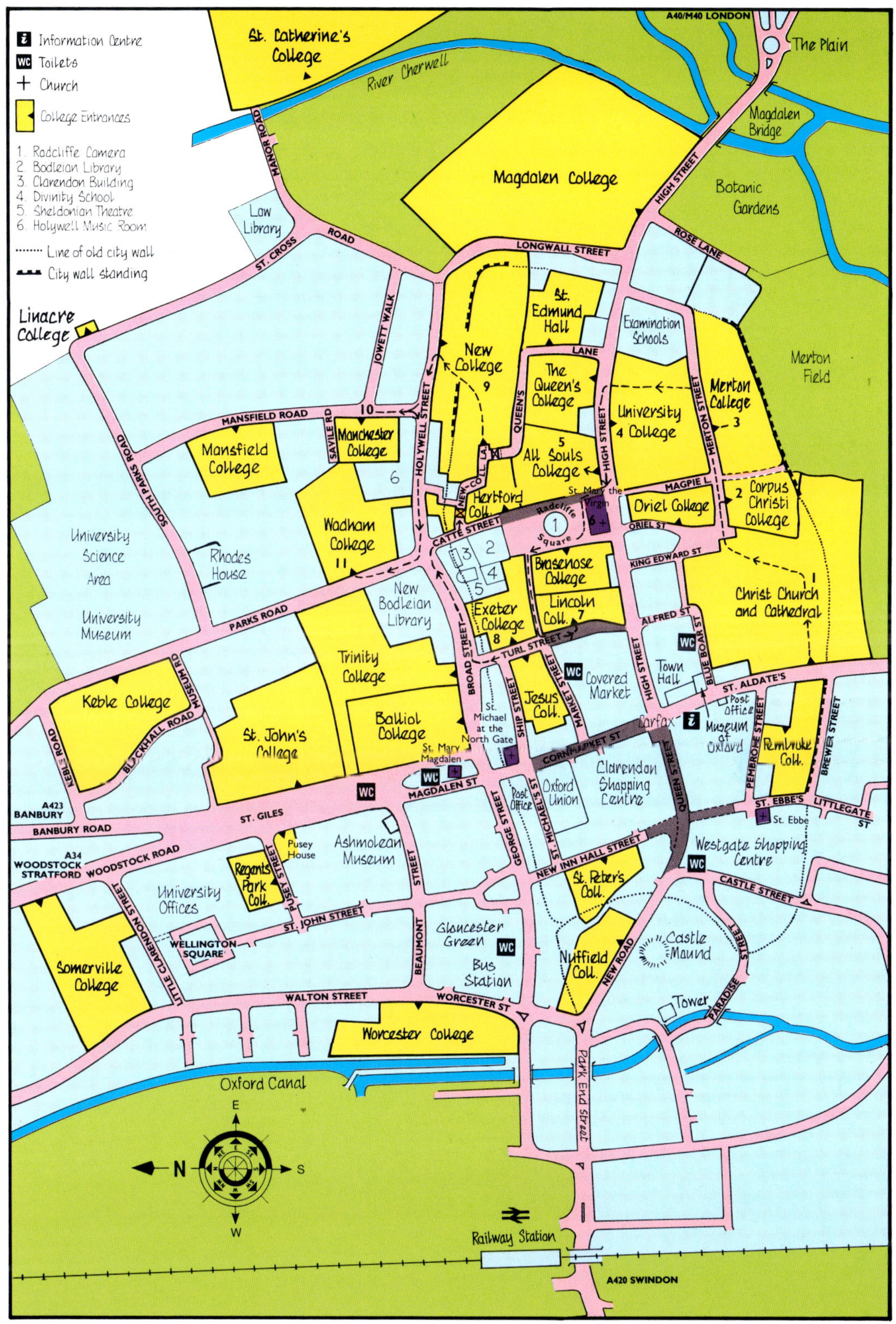
Information Centre
Toilets
Church
College Entrances
1. Radcliffe Camera
2. Bodleian Library
3. Clarendon Building
4. Divinity School
5. Sheldonian Theatre
6. Holywell Music Room
Line of old city wall
City wall standing
St. Catherine's College
River Cherwell
A40/M40 LONDON
The Plain
Magdalen Bridge
Magdalen College
Botanic Gardens
Law Library
Linacre College
MANOR ROAD
ST. CROSS ROAD
LONGWALL STREET
ROSE LANE
HIGH STREET
St. Edmund Hall
New College
Examination Schools
Merton Field
Merton College
JOWETT WALK
The Queen's College
QUEEN'S LANE
University College
MERTON STREET
MANSFIELD ROAD
SAVILE RD
Manchester College
HOLYWELL STREET
NEW COLL. LA.
All Souls College
Mansfield College
SOUTH PARKS ROAD
Hertford Coll.
St. Mary the Virgin
MAGPIE L.
Oriel College
ORIEL ST
Corpus Christi College
Radcliffe Square
CATTE STREET
Wadham College
University Science Area
Rhodes House
KING EDWARD ST
Brasenose College
Christ Church and Cathedral
New Bodleian Library
Exeter College
Lincoln Coll.
University Museum
PARKS ROAD
ALFRED ST
TURL STREET
BLUE BOAR ST
Trinity College
Town Hall
Covered Market
BROAD STREET
MUSEUM RD
Keble College
KEBLE ROAD
BLACKHALL ROAD
St. John's College
Balliol College
St. Michael at the North Gate
SHIP STREET
Jesus Coll.
MARKET STREET
ST. ALDATE'S
Carfax
Post Office
Museum of Oxford
PEMBROKE STREET
Pembroke Coll.
BREWER STREET
St. Mary Magdalen
CORNMARKET ST
Clarendon Shopping Centre
QUEEN STREET
A423 BANBURY
BANBURY ROAD
ST. GILES
MAGDALEN ST
Post Office
Oxford Union
ST. MICHAEL'S ST
ST. EBBE'S
St. Ebbe
LITTLEGATE ST
A34 WOODSTOCK STRATFORD
WOODSTOCK ROAD
Pusey House
Ashmolean Museum
GEORGE STREET
NEW INN HALL STREET
Westgate Shopping Centre
Regent's Park Coll.
PUSEY STREET
University Offices
ST. JOHN STREET
St. Peter's Coll.
CASTLE STREET
LITTLE CLARENDON STREET
WELLINGTON SQUARE
BEAUMONT STREET
Gloucester Green
Bus Station
Nuffield Coll.
NEW ROAD
Castle Mound
PARADISE STREET
Somerville College
WALTON STREET
WORCESTER ST
Tower
Worcester College
Oxford Canal
Park End Street
E
N
S
W
Railway Station
A420 SWINDON

THE GAZETTEER

How To Use The Gazetteer
Churches and college chapels are listed alphabetically. Each entry has a brief note on the architectural history of the building, followed by a résumé of the glass it contains. Windows are then listed in a clockwise direction, starting at the altar end, and are indicated with arabic numerals. Clerestory windows are indicated with Roman capital letters. The subject matter of each window is briefly described from top to bottom, left to right, starting with the tracery at the top. Subjects within a light are separated by a hyphen; the lights are subdivided using a semi-colon. Heraldry is not on the whole identified. Indications of artist, workshop and date are given where known. Glass no longer in existence or in store is not described. A pair of binoculars is a valuable tool for seeing the stained glass.

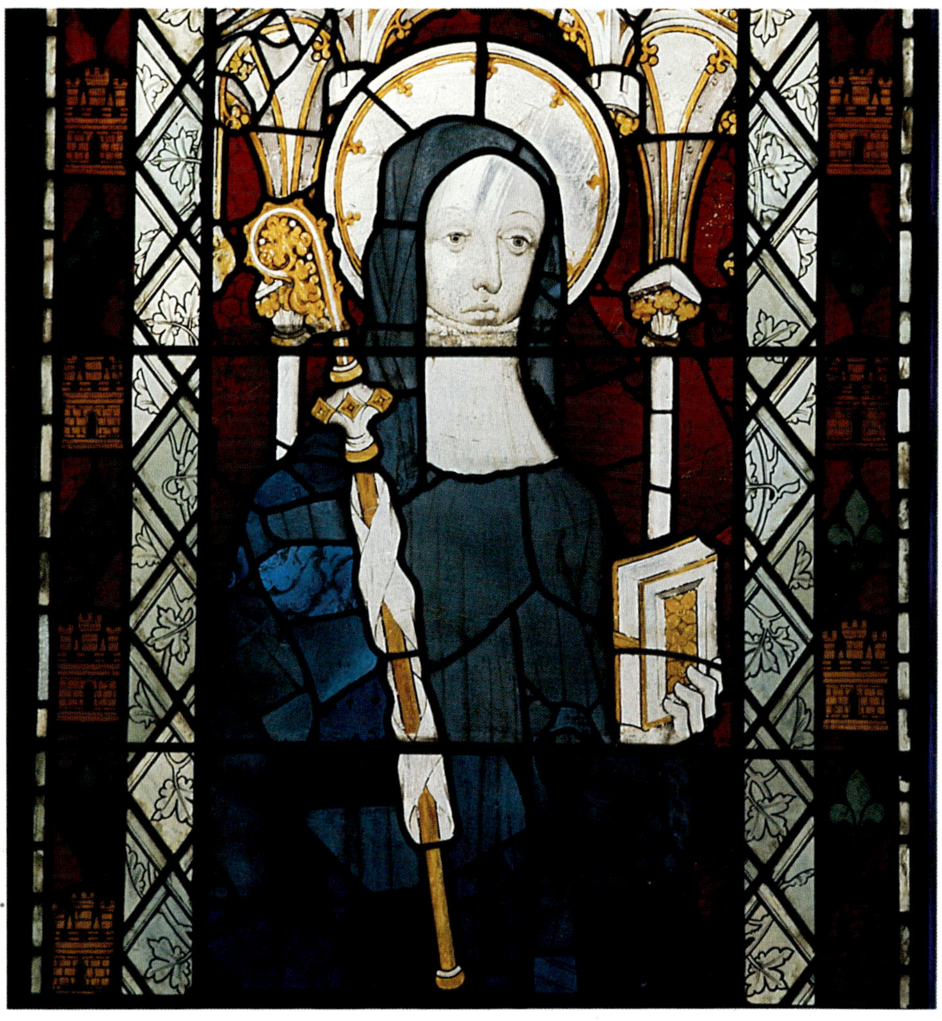

Fig. 34. *A saintly Benedictine Abbess, one of the few remaining fragments of the late 14th/15th-century transept glazing. (Merton College Chapel, window 1)*

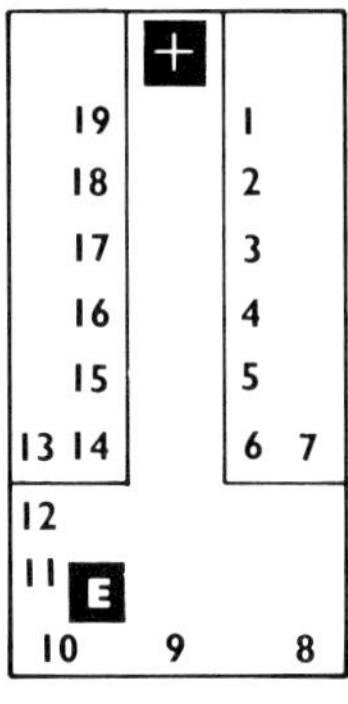

ALL SOULS COLLEGE CHAPEL

The college was founded jointly by Henry Chichele, Archbishop of Canterbury, and King Henry VI. In scale and richness, the architecture reflects the dignity of its royal patron and the ambitions of its archiepiscopal founder, who had himself been one of Wykeham's New College scholars. The chapel is entered by a beautifully vaulted passage. The foundations were begun on 10 February 1438; the chapel was consecrated in 1442.

Glass: Windows 6-8 and 10-14, workshop of JOHN GLASIER and others, mid-15th century. Window 9, JOHN HARDMAN & CO, 1861, and 1-5 and 15-19, CLAYTON & BELL, 1870s. Window 12, plain.

1-5, CLAYTON & BELL, 1870s

1. *Tracery: Apostles. The Betrayal of Christ in the Garden; Christ in the Temple with the Doctors*
2. *Tracery: Angels. Centurion Cornelius — The Baptism of Candace's Eunuch; St Stephen — Sacred female giving alms; St John the Baptist — St Luke*
3. *Tracery: Angels. Daniel — Sacred male talking to architect/builder; Jonah — Sacred male addressing a crowd; Solomon — Supervision of transport of timber*
4. *Tracery: Angels. Job — Priests blowing trumpets; St Anne — Samson destroying the Temple; Samuel — David playing his harp*
5. *Tracery: Angels. Jacob — probably Moses' childhood in Egypt; Isaac — probably Moses distributing corn; Abraham — Building of Noah's ark*

6-8 and 10-14: The medieval building accounts show that on 13 May 1441 JOHN GLASIER of Oxford was paid for the glazing of the eight windows of the chapel. In 1447 he was paid for the west window (9) of the antechapel. Another payment in 1441 was made to JOHN PROWTE (*sic*), glazier. This was JOHN PRUDDE of Westminster, the King's Glazier, appointed by Henry VI, joint patron of All Souls. It has been suggested that his workshop painted the female saints in the antechapel, which are in a rather different style to the apostles. The 15th-century glass in windows 8, 10 and 11 was removed from the library in 1750.

6. *Tracery: Angels. St James Minor with falchion — St Elizabeth with the young St John the Baptist; St Philip holding a small cross — St Helen holding the True Cross; St Bartholomew with flaying knife — St Agatha*
7. *Tracery: Angels. St Jude with fuller's club — St Etheldreda; St Simon with three loaves — St Catherine with spiked wheel and sword; St Matthias with axe — St Sidwell (labelled 'Sativola') with the scythe of her martyrdom*
8. *A series of 12 royal figures, originally located in the library (tracery figures by CLAYTON & BELL). King Constantine — King Aelred — St Edward Martyr — King Edward II; St Ethelbert — King Athelstan — King Canute — John of Gaunt; St Oswald — King Edgar — St Edward the Confessor — Henry V*
9. *JOHN HARDMAN & CO, designed by JOHN HARDMAN POWELL, 1861. A 7-light 'Doom' window, with the Archangel Michael dividing the Righteous Souls from the Damned.*
10. *A series of 12 Bishops and Doctors of the Church, originally located in the library (tracery figures by CLAYTON & BELL). St Cyprian — St Dunstan — St Ambrose — St Augustine; St Augustine of Canterbury — St Oswald — John Stratford, Archbishop of Canterbury — Archbishop Henry Chichele (modern); St John of Beverley — St Alphege — St Jerome — St Gregory*
11. *(Above door) Six figures, originally located in the library (tracery figures by BETTON & EVANS). St Edmund — King Henry VI; St Dunstan — Archbishop Henry Chichele; Odo, Archbishop of Canterbury — King Arthur*
12.
13. *Tracery: Angels. St Peter holding keys — St Anne teaching the young Virgin Mary to read; St Andrew holding his cross — The Virgin and Child; St James Major dressed as a pilgrim — St Mary Cleophas with her children (St Simon, St Joseph & St James Minor)*
14. *Tracery: Angels. St John the Evangelist with chalice and viper — St Mary Salome with her children (St John the Evangelist & St James Major); St Thomas with spear — St Mary Magdalene with jar of ointment; St Matthew with scimitar — St Anastasia*

15-19, CLAYTON & BELL, 1870s

15. *Tracery: Angels. Abel — Sacred man with tent and sheep; Enoch — David playing harp; Methusaleh — Sacred man with a blacksmith*
16. *Tracery: Angels. Aaron — Priests making burnt offering; Gideon — Martial angel appears to Gideon; Elijah — Restoration to life of the widow's son*
17. *Tracery: Angels. Hezekiah — Sacred man disputing with a crowd; Ezekiel — Reads from a scroll to a young king; Manasseh — Dictates to a scribe*
18. *Tracery: Angels. Barnabas — Old man instructs a young man; Mark — The Virgin, St Anne and Christ; Apollos — St John the Evangelist*
19. *Tracery: Apostles. A single scene showing Christ flanked by Moses and St John the Evangelist; Christ with the Virgin Mary and St Joseph in the carpenter's shop*

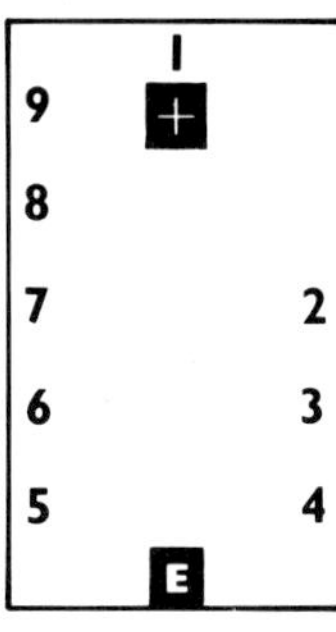

BALLIOL COLLEGE CHAPEL

Founded in the 13th century, the college is one of the oldest in Oxford, although its present buildings date principally from the 19th century. The impressive Broad Street frontage was designed by Alfred Waterhouse, also known for his civic buildings in his native Manchester. The chapel was rebuilt 1856-7 to designs by William Butterfield on the site of the medieval chapel, which was finished in 1529.

Glass: Windows 1-3, 6 and 7, mostly 1529. Windows 4, 5, 8 and 9, ABRAHAM VAN LINGE, 1637. The glass was reset *c.*1910 by HUGH ARNOLD, a pupil of CHRISTOPHER WHALL.

1. *The Passion of Christ, 1529. Disturbed remains of original 5-light window given by Lawrence Stubbs and his brother Richard (Master of the College), who appear at the base of the window and whose initials appear in the tracery trefoils. The main subject of the window is Christ's Passion. The Betrayal — The Agony in the Garden — St Lawrence — Angel with shield; Christ carrying the Cross — The Crowning with Thorns — The Flagellation — Lawrence Stubbs; The Crucifixion — Pilate washing his hands — Panel of fragments; The arrest of Christ — Ecce Homo — Pietà — Richard Stubbs; The Ascension — The Resurrection — St Augustine of Hippo — Angel with shield*
2. *Scenes from the life of St Catherine, 1529. One of the better preserved windows in the chapel, also given by Lawrence and Richard Stubbs. St Catherine prays before the torture wheel — St Catherine converting the Empress; St Catherine scourged — St Catherine enthroned ; St Catherine beheaded — St Catherine buried on Mount Sinai by Angels*
3. *Composite figures, c.1529. St Hugh of Lincoln — The Virgin Mary (probably from a Crucifixion); Panel of fragments with male head — St Lawrence (head lost) — St Edward the Confessor; Part of St Mary Magdalene — St Frideswide*
4. *ABRAHAM VAN LINGE, 1637. The Baptism of Candace's Eunuch.*
5. *Inscribed 'ABRAHAM VAN LINGE FECIT 163-'. St Philip preaching to the Eunuch, seated in his chariot.*
6. *Composite figures, c.1529. St John the Evangelist — St Michael fighting the dragon; The Virgin and Child — St Anthony Abbot (badly disturbed) — St John the Evangelist (probably from a Crucifixion); St John the Evangelist — St Margaret emerging from the belly of the dragon*
7. *Composite panels, mostly 16th century, gathered from a number of different windows. Panel of fragments — Virgin Mary adoring the Christ Child (head only, 16th century) — John Hygden, President of Magdalen College; Two shields from the Compton window (1530) — Thomas Chase, Master of Balliol 1421-8 and eight Fellows of the college — Sir William Compton and his two sons; Panel of red fragments — Panel probably by ABRAHAM VAN LINGE — Thomas Knolles, Subdean of York. Fragments of inscription at the base of the lights refer to Richard Atkins, who gave a window to the medieval chapel.*
8. *ABRAHAM VAN LINGE, 1637. A crowd outside the palace of King Hezekiah.*
9. *Inscribed 'ABRAHAM VAN LINGE FECIT 1637'. The sickness and recovery of King Hezekiah.*

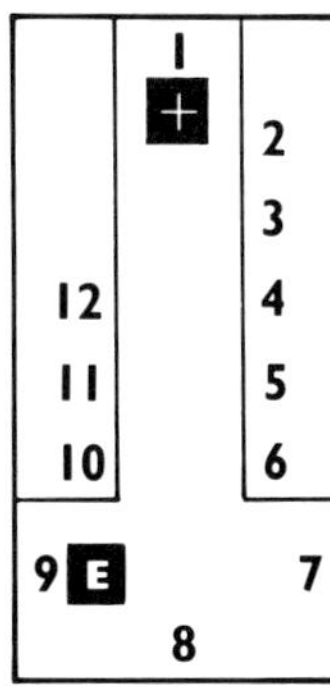

BRASENOSE COLLEGE CHAPEL

The college was founded in 1509 on the site of an earlier foundation. Its pleasant intimacy of scale offers a marked contrast to the public grandeur of the Radcliffe Camera next to it. The chapel was begun in 1656 and consecrated in 1666. No glass survives from this period, although the painted gothic vault with pendants is an impressive reminder of its earlier history.

Glass: Windows 1-5, 7, 9 (C E KEMPE, WILLIAM WAILES, JAMES POWELL & SON, CLAYTON & BELL), 19th century. Window 8, JAMES PEARSON after J H MORTIMER, 1776. Windows 6, 10 and 11, plain.

1. *CHARLES EAMER KEMPE, 1896. Tracery: The Sacred Monogram; Cherub heads. The large figures in the main lights have half-length figures of prophets in niches beneath them. A bishop; Isaiah; The Virgin Mary — Jeremiah; The Crucifixion — David; St John the Evangelist — Zachariah; Figure in armour — Micah*
2. *WILLIAM WAILES, c.1850. Tracery: The Parable of the Sower. The Pentecost*
3. *WILLIAM WAILES, 1855. Tracery: Dives and Lazarus. The Last Supper — Abraham and Melchisedek; The Miracle of the Loaves and Fishes; The Crucifixion — The Sacrifice of Isaac*
4. *WILLIAM WAILES, 1849. Tracery: probably Joseph's Dream. The Entombment — Joseph cast into the Well; The Resurrection; The three Marys at the empty tomb —*

Joseph and the Merchants
5. *WILLIAM WAILES, 1864. Tracery: probably Aaron. The Transfiguration — Hezekiel raised up by angels; The Ascension; Christ's charge to Peter — Elijah and Elisha*
7. *JAMES POWELL & SONS, probably designed by HARRY ELLIS WOOLDRIDGE, 1887. Tracery: Angels with shields. St Cedda; Virgin and Child; St Michael the Archangel; St Hugh*
8. *Christ and the Four Evangelists, painted by JAMES PEARSON after JOHN HAMILTON MORTIMER, dated 1776. Surround 19th century. Inscribed (under Matthew's foot) 'I. PEARSON FECIT 1776'.*
9. *CLAYTON & BELL, 1894. Tracery: Angels. St John the Baptist — Baptism of Christ; St Paul — St Paul preaching at Athens; St Peter — Christ's charge to Peter; St John the Evangelist — St John and the Virgin Mary*
12. *WILLIAM WAILES, 1862. Tracery: St Paul preaching at Athens. St Paul, with four scenes from his life.*

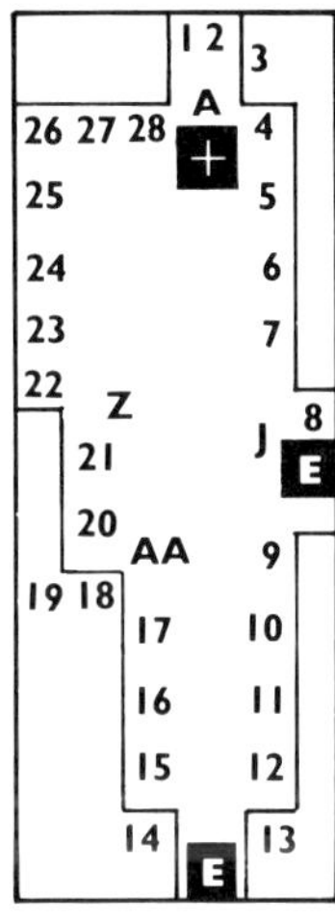

CHRIST CHURCH

The most spacious and gracious of the Oxford colleges. Tom Quad with its elegant Mercury Fountain, is the largest in Oxford, reflecting the pride and ambition of the college's founder, Cardinal Wolsey. The tower was completed by Sir Christopher Wren. In fact, the architectural history of Christ Church begins long before the creation of Wolsey's Cardinal College in 1525. The college stands on the site of the Augustinian priory of St Frideswide, the cathedral having once been the priory church. The earliest part of the cathedral dates from the late 12th century, although the Latin and Lucy Chapels are 14th-century additions. In 1524 the priory was suppressed by Wolsey and some of the west end of the church (about 50 ft) was demolished to accommodate Tom Quad, the first stage of his projected reconstruction of the site. Wolsey's fall from favour put a halt to the demolition work, thus preserving most of the medieval fabric. Henry VIII adopted Wolsey's project, making the priory church first the college chapel and later (1546) the cathedral.

THE CATHEDRAL

Glass: Windows 8, 21-23, 14th century. Windows 7, 14, 18-20 (traceries), ABRAHAM VAN LINGE. Windows 1, 2, 4-6, 9-13, 16, 17, 21-28, A, J (CLAYTON & BELL , JOHN HARDMAN & CO, JAMES POWELL & SONS, WILLIAM WAILES, MORRIS, MARSHALL FAULKNER & CO), 19th century. Windows 3, 15, 29 and most of the clerestory, plain.

1. *CLAYTON & BELL, 1875. Christ carrying the Cross — Christ's entry into Jerusalem*
2. *CLAYTON & BELL, 1875. The three Marys at the empty tomb — The Entombment*
4. *MORRIS & CO, designed by EDWARD BURNE-JONES, 1878. Tracery: Angels with musical instruments. Angel of Victory — St Catherine in the Temple; St Catherine — St Catherine's vision of the Virgin Mary; Angel of Suffering — Entombment of St Catherine*
5. *JOHN HARDMAN & CO, designed by JOHN HARDMAN POWELL, 1870s. The Vision of St John on Patmos.*
6. *JOHN HARDMAN & CO, designed by JOHN HARDMAN POWELL, 1870s. The Vision of Ezekiel.*
7. *Bishop Robert King with the ruins of Osney Abbey, probably by ABRAHAM VAN LINGE, 1630-40.*
8. ***Chapel of St Lucy:*** *This window is remarkable for the retention of its early 14th-century tracery lights relatively intact. In its fascinating mixture of the sacred and the profane, it closely resembles the sort of decoration favoured in illuminated manuscripts of the same date. The glass is characterized by a great richness of colour and by the use of a variety of background designs. The upper, smaller openings use a leaf motif picked out of a layer of paint, while the larger quatrefoil openings use either a trellis-like device or a series of wavy stars set in medallions. The scenes are described in tiers, starting at the apex of the window.*
*i. (Apex) Christ in Majesty **ii.** Censing angel; Censing angel **iii.** Kneeling donor; Arms of France; Arms of England; Kneeling donor **iv.** Grotesque creature with rabbit's head; 2-headed grotesque; Grotesque with female head and foliage tail; Grotesque youth; Grotesque centaur with drum and horn; Grotesque lion with axe **v.** Grotesque animal with green head; Grotesque bull with wings; Lewd naked woman; Grotesque naked man with spear; Grotesque dragon; Bird of prey **vi.** St Augustine preaching; The martyrdom of St Thomas Becket (head of St Thomas lost); St Martin of Tours dividing his cloak with a beggar **vii.** Head of a queen; St Blaise; St Cuthbert holding the head of St Oswald; Head of a king*
The borders of the main lights are filled with fragments of all dates. A series of quatrefoils and triangular

shapes in the centre of the lights has been filled with fragments, mostly 19th century, but with some important medieval pieces. Quatrefoil with 19th-century head — Triangle containing late 16th/early 17th-century Netherlandish roundel of a feast scene — Quatrefoil with 19th-century head; Triangle with 14th-century tonsured male head — Large quatrefoil with 14th-century kneeling tonsured male donor, hands raised in prayer — Triangle with 18th-century God in the clouds; Quatrefoil with 19th-century head — Triangle with 17th-century armorial — Quatrefoil with 19th-century head

9. *CLAYTON & BELL, 1872. Tracery: Angels. Samuel and Eli — The Wise and Foolish Virgins; The Crossing of the Red Sea — Christ walking on the Sea of Galilee; The Vision of Isaiah — The walk to Emmaus*
10. *CLAYTON & BELL, 1870. Tracery: Angels with emblems of the Passion. Probably Saul and David — St Paul in Prison; The Virgin Mary and St Joseph — The Betrayal of Christ; Christ before the High Priest — St Paul and St Luke*
11. *JAMES POWELL & SONS, designed by JAMES E ROGERS, 1864. The Life of St Peter.*
12. *(Above door) WILLIAM WAILES, 1858. Tracery: Angels playing musical instruments. St Peter healing a child; The Crucifixion; Christ healing a sick man*
13. *MORRIS, MARSHALL FAULKNER & CO, designed by EDWARD BURNE-JONES and WILLIAM MORRIS, 1871. Tracery: Seraphs and angels with musical instruments (designed by Morris). Main light figures designed by Burne-Jones: Hope; Charity; Faith*
14. *Jonah seated beneath the gourd with the city of Nineveh before him. Inscribed 'ABRAHAM VAN LINGE FECIT 163(-)'.*
16. *CLAYTON & BELL, 1874. Tracery: Angels with instruments of the Passion. Scenes from the life of St Stephen.*
17. *CLAYTON & BELL, 1873. Tracery: Angels. Abraham and Melchizedek — Jesus and Nicodemus; King David — Christ's charge to St Peter; Moses — Christ appearing to St Thomas*

18-20: Tracery lights only, probably by ABRAHAM VAN LINGE, 1630-40.

18. *A city with a burning building.*
19. *A city on fire.*
20. *A city.*
21. *CLAYTON & BELL, 1875. Tracery: Angels with shields. St Michael the Archangel and the Angelic Host at the Last Judgement.*

22-24: ***Latin Chapel,*** second quarter of the 14th century. All three windows have undergone restoration, especially in their borders and grisaille.

22. *Tracery: Shield at apex, head of king, head of bishop. Foliage backgrounds. Each of the three main lights contains a large standing female figure framed by a well-developed, turreted canopy. Borders are filled with an alternation of climbing naturalistic foliage and fleur-de-lis devices. The quarries of trailing oak leaves are heavily restored. St Catherine, with wheel and sword; The Virgin and Child, the Christ Child holding a globe; probably St Hilda. All three figures are crowned and have vestigial inscriptions at their feet.*
23. *Tracery: two male heads. The arrangement of the three figures in this window is not original — the outer lights are by a different and coarser hand than the central figure which is closer to the female saints in windows 22 and 24. To the left is the angel Gabriel with the message 'Ave Maria' and to the right is the Virgin Mary — read together the figures depict the Annunciation. The central light contains a figure of an archbishop saint, painted on a larger scale and in a rather more refined style. The borders of the outer lights are all restoration, but those of the centre light contain a fascinating selection of grotesques, monkeys and birds.*
24. *Tracery: all restoration, except for the dove descending in the apex. A companion window to 22, although with more attenuated canopies topped with 'spires'. The outer borders are filled with naturalistic climbing foliage, mostly restoration, that of the centre light with an alternation of lion masks and fleurs-de-lis, mostly original. St Margaret spearing the dragon; St Frideswide, patroness and founder of the priory; St Catherine (her second appearance). All three figures are crowned and labelled.*
25. *CLAYTON & BELL, c.1890. Tracery: Angels holding shields. St Mary Magdalene; St John the Evangelist; St Frideswide*
26. *JAMES POWELL & SONS, designed by EDWARD BURNE-JONES, 1859. Tracery: A ship, above scenes of the Tree of Knowledge and Adam and Eve, and smaller roundels with angels. St Frideswide and her companions with St Cecilia and St Catherine — St Frideswide founds her first convent — St Frideswide demanded in marriage by the King of Mercia and the dispersal of her community; St Frideswide flees to Abingdon pursued by the King and his followers — She hides in a pigsty; Pursued by the King, St Frideswide takes refuge at Binsey — The convent at Binsey and the Saint's acts of Mercy; St Frideswide returns to Oxford but the city is besieged by the King of Mercia, who is struck blind — The death of St Frideswide*
27. *MORRIS, MARSHALL, FAULKNER & CO, designed by EDWARD BURNE-JONES and WILLIAM MORRIS, 1872-3 (The Vyner Memorial window). Tracery: Angels with harps. Samuel — Samuel and Eli; David — David slays Goliath; St John the Evangelist — St John lays his head on Christ's breast; Timothy — Timothy and Eunice (Vyner was a Christ Church undergraduate murdered by Greek brigands in 1870 at the age of only 23.)*
28. *MORRIS, MARSHALL, FAULKNER & CO, designed by EDWARD BURNE-JONES and WILLIAM MORRIS, 1875. Tracery: Angels with musical instruments (Morris). Main light figures designed by Burne-Jones: Angel holding a lyre and palm — The conversion of Valerian; St Cecilia — St Cecilia sends the angel to Valerian; Angel with violin and palm — The martyrdom of St Cecilia*

A. *CLAYTON & BELL, 1875. Rose window: Christ in Majesty surrounded by Angels.*

J. *CLAYTON & BELL, 1891. The Tree of Jesse (a pictorial interpretation of the genealogy of Christ).*

Z. *(Tracery blank) A jumble of buildings, landscape and men's heads, probably by ABRAHAM VAN LINGE, 1630-40.*

AA. *(Tracery blank) Angels playing instruments, landscape, heads and a jumble of buildings, probably by ABRAHAM VAN LINGE, 1630-40.*

Central Tower: *The eight lancet windows contain richly coloured fragments of all dates, mostly post-medieval, leaded into geometric patterns.*

THE CHAPTER HOUSE

Glass: 15th, early 16th century, and 17th century.

Window facing entrance: *17th-century enamelled armorials. Windows in the right-hand wall contain fragmentary late 15th- and early 16th-century glass. The most important panels show the Virgin and Child, a figure of a cardinal, the arms of Wolsey, the Assumption of the Virgin Mary and a lily pot from an Annunciation. The panel depicting Pilate washing his hands is probably of Netherlandish origin. Staircase window (to R of entrance): Interesting 15th-century fragments, worthy of close examination. At both top and bottom are large M (for Maria) monograms. The strokes of the letters are decorated with the Assumption of the Virgin supported by angels. The central monogram is of IHC and the strokes of the letters are here painted with the Cruxifixion flanked by the Virgin Mary and St John with the instruments of the Passion. At the base of the Cross is a hell-mouth with a soul issuing from it.*

THE GREAT HALL

Glass: Window 1, early 16th century. Windows 2 and 16, BURLISON & GRYLLS, 1880s. Windows 3-15, PATRICK REYNTIENS, 1983. Window 17, 17th- and 18th-century armorials.

1. Above dais: A number of early 16th-century shields of arms survives, heavily restored, from Cardinal Wolsey's Cardinal College, created out of St Frideswide's Priory in 1524. Badges and shields of arms relating to Wolsey's numerous ecclesiastical possessions, including the archbishopric of York, bishoprics of Durham, Winchester and Rochester. His monogram and personal badges can also be seen. Further examples in windows 2 and 16. The arms of Henry VIII also survive.

3-15, PATRICK REYNTIENS, 1983. A series of windows with heraldry and inscriptions, incorporating portraits of distinguished Christ Church men, notably C L Dodgson (better known as Lewis Carroll), with characters from the Alice books.

2 and 16, BURLISON & GRYLLS, 1880s. Founders, benefactors and scholars of the college.

17. 17th- and 18th-century armorials.

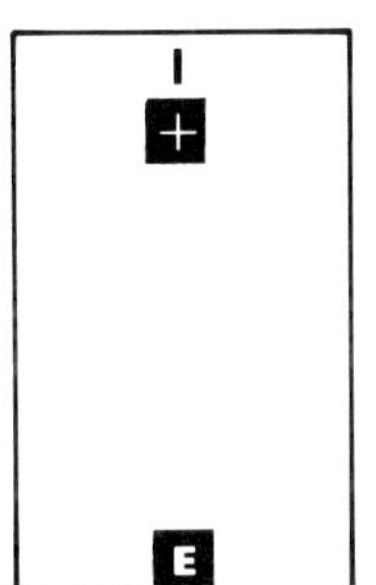

CORPUS CHRISTI COLLEGE CHAPEL

One of the smallest and most intimate of the colleges. A memorable feature is the impressive sundial, surmounted by the college emblem, the pelican. The chapel was built 1512-17, although it was slightly enlarged in 1676 and re-roofed in 1843. No stained glass survives from the foundation period. It contains the only window in the Arts and Crafts tradition within the city, which presides over an otherwise plain-glazed chapel.

1. HENRY A PAYNE, 1931. St Christopher with the Christ Child in the foreground of a seascape with sailing ships, the heavenly City beyond. In the upper part of the centre lights, a vision of the Blessed Sacrament with Angels.

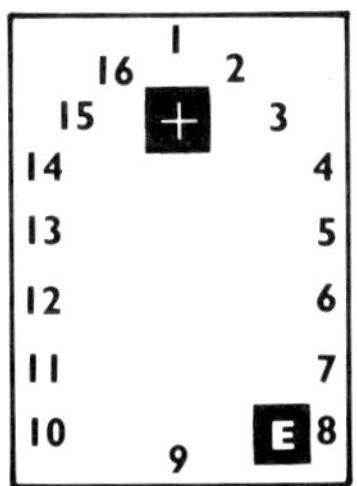

EXETER COLLEGE CHAPEL

The college was founded in 1314; Sir George Gilbert Scott's sumptuous chapel (1856-60), inspired by the Sainte Chapelle in Paris, is the very epitome of the Gothic Revival, faithful to its French model in the richness, delicacy and verticality of its execution.

Glass: All windows by CLAYTON & BELL, 1859-*c.*1890. All except 8 and 9 have figures of angels in the tracery lights and between the principal subject panels. Windows 10 and 11, plain.

1. 1859/60. Moses and the Brazen Serpent — The Manna in the Wilderness; The Crucifixion — The Last Supper

2. 1859/60. Elijah and Elisha — Elisha and the Priests of Baal; The Ascension — Pentecost

3. 1859/60. Crossing of the Red Sea — Moses receiving the Tablets of the Law; The Baptism of Christ — The Temptation of Christ

4. 1860. Six scenes from the Life of St Peter.

5. Mid-1860s. The Acts of the Apostles, including St Stephen and St Philip.

6. c.1870. Six scenes from the life of St Paul.

7. c.1870. The Vision of St John the Evangelist on Patmos.

8. c.1890. King David; Angel; Jubal

9. Probably c.1890. Rose window with heraldry.

12. 1880s. Ruth and Boaz — Gideon with the fleece; Samuel and David — Miriam; David and Goliath — Samson

13. 1880s. Elisha and the priests of Baal — The Judgement of King Solomon; probably King David — Saul; probably Jonah — probably The death of David

14. 1880s. Psalm 137 — Daniel in the lions' den; The three men in the fiery furnace — Belshazzar's feast; Ezekiel in the Valley of Dry Bones — Judas Maccabaeus

15. 1859/60. The birth of St John the Baptist — Zacharias and the Angel; The Nativity — The Annunciation

16. 1859/60. Joseph and the Merchants — Joseph cast into the pit; The Resurrection — The Entombment

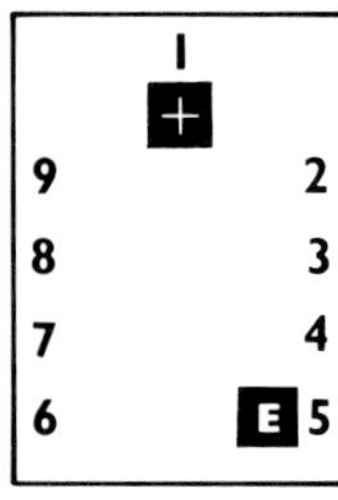

JESUS COLLEGE CHAPEL

Jesus College is famous for its unbreakable links with Wales, a connection reflected in many of its chapel windows. The college was founded in 1571, but the most substantial buildings date from the 17th and 18th centuries. The chapel was begun *c.*1617; the chancel was added in 1636.

Glass: Window 1, GEORGE HEDGELAND, 1856. Window 2, CLAYTON & BELL, 1874. Windows 4 and 7, C E KEMPE, 1890s. Window 9, LAVERS & WESTLAKE. Windows 3, 5, 6 and 8, plain.

1. *GEORGE HEDGELAND, 1856. Tracery: Christ in Majesty with angels. Three Miracle scenes below The Nativity — The Creation of Adam; The Baptism of Christ — The Crossing of the Red Sea; The Last Supper — The First Passover; The Crucifixion — Moses and the Brazen Serpent; The Resurrection — Jonah and the Whale; Christ appearing to the Disciples in the Upper Room — Samuel and David; The Ascension — Elijah and Elisha*
2. *CLAYTON & BELL, 1874. Tracery: Angels. The Adoration of the Christ Child by the Magi and Shepherds. Below are small scenes of the Annunciation, Nativity and Presentation in the Temple.*
4. *CHARLES EAMER KEMPE, 1890s. Tracery: Angels. St Cyfelyn; Archbishop Laud; St Padern*
7. *CHARLES EAMER KEMPE, 1897. Tracery: Angels. St Asaph; St David; St Deiniol*
9. *LAVERS & WESTLAKE, designed by NATHANIEL H J WESTLAKE. Tracery: Symbols of Faith, Hope and Charity. St Peter — St Peter walks on water; Christ — Christ calms a storm; St Paul*

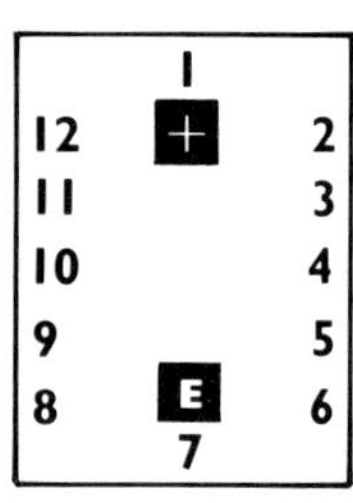

KEBLE COLLEGE CHAPEL

Keble was built to designs by William Butterfield, 1868-82, as a monument to the Oxford Movement. Its robust brick and stone architecture, enlivened with polychrome detail, is in surprising and lively contrast to Oxford's usual limestone. The chapel is a vast space in which the richly coloured figures in the windows stand way above the heads of the congregation.

Glass: All windows designed and made by ALEXANDER GIBBS (closely supervised by Butterfield), 1873-4.

1. *Christ with the 12 disciples and the Virgin Mary.*
2. *St John Chrysostom; St Basil*
3. *St Athanasius; St Gregory Nazianzus*
4. *(Obscured by organ) St Matthew; St Peter; St Mark*
5. *Nahum; Habakkuk; Zephaniah*
6. *Haggai; Zachariah; Malachi*
7. *Isaiah; Samuel — Jeremiah; Solomon — David; Elijah — Ezekiel; Daniel*
8. *Hosea; Joel; Amos*
9. *Obadiah; Jonah; Micah*
10. *St Luke; St Paul; St John the Evangelist*
11. *St Jerome; St Ambrose*
12. *St Gregory the Great; St Augustine of Hippo*

Side Chapel *(entrance to R of altar): CHARLES EAMER KEMPE, c.1900. Virgin and Child. The chapel also contains W Holman Hunt's famous painting, 'The Light of the World'.*

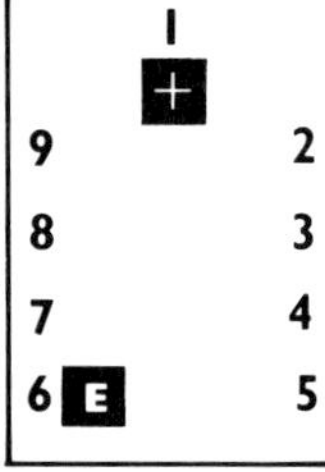

LINCOLN COLLEGE CHAPEL

The college was founded as the College of the Blessed Mary and All Saints, Lincoln in 1427. The chapel, built 1629-31, has a greater sense of privacy than almost any other Oxford college, being situated not in the first, but the second quadrangle. The massive figures in the windows are well suited to its simple barrel-like space.

Glass: Windows all probably by ABRAHAM VAN LINGE, 1629, 1630 and 1631.

1. *Antitypes from the New Testament and the Types which were thought to prefigure them, dated 1631. Tracery: Elevations of classical buildings. The Nativity — The Creation of Adam and Eve; The Baptism of Christ — The Crossing of the Red Sea; The Last Supper — The Feast of the Passover; The Crucifixion — The Brazen Serpent; The Resurrection — Jonah and the Whale; The Ascension — The Ascent of Elijah*

2-5: Apostles, dated 1629 and 1630. Traceries: Angels holding shields.

2. *St Peter (1629); St Andrew; St James Major*
3. *St John; St Philip; St Bartholomew (1630)*
4. *St Matthew (1630); St Thomas (1630); St James Minor*
5. *St Jude; St Simon; St Matthias (1630)*

6-9: Prophets. Traceries: Angels holding shields.

6. *Obadiah; Jonah, Elisha*
7. *Malachi; Zachariah; Amos*
8. *Ezekiel; Jeremiah; Isaiah*
9. *Elijah; Daniel; David*

MAGDALEN COLLEGE CHAPEL

Magdalen is the very epitome of an Oxford college, its buildings attractively grouped, and the whole beautifully sited from whichever direction it is approached. Magdalen stands on the banks of the River Cherwell, giving its name to one of Oxford's principal bridges. Its lovely tower is one of the city's best known landmarks. Founded in 1458 by William of Waynflete, Bishop of Winchester; the chapel was built 1474-80.

Glass: Window outside chapel entrance — some medieval fragments. Windows 6-10 and 12-14, RICHARD GREENBURY, 1632. Windows 1-5 and 15-19, JOHN HARDMAN & CO, 1857-60. Window 11, plain.

Window outside chapel entrance: *Some trails of 14th-century oak leaf grisaille and pieces of 15th-century architecture. Most important is the partial male head (late 15th century) and part of a bishop's crozier.*

Chapel

1-5, JOHN HARDMAN & CO, 1857-60

1. *Tracery: Angels. St Cecilia; St Frideswide*
2. *Tracery: Angels. St Simon — St Ambrose; St Hieronymus — St Gregory; St Augustus — St Quadratus*
3. *Tracery: Angels. St Philip — St Melito; St Barnabas — St Justinian; St Birinus — St Stephen*
4. *Tracery: Angels. St Melitius — Ephraim; St Michael — Gabriel; Theophilus — St Christopher*
5. *Tracery: Angels. St Matthew — St Simon; St Thomas — St Jude; St James Major — St Matthias*

6-10 and 12-14: These windows were probably painted by RICHARD GREENBURY in 1632. The tracery lights of all of them contain cherubs or seraphs, with two tiers of figures below.

6. *St Cornelius — St Basil; St Clement of Alexandria — St Gregory; St Cyprian — St Cyril*
7. *St Julius — St Clement; St Polycarp — St Timothy; St Ignatius — St Irenaeus*
8. *St Mary Magdalene — St Agnes; St Mary the Virgin — St Theodosia; St Anne — St Eulalia*
9. *St Gregory of Nyssa — St Hippolytus; St George — St Nicholas; St Cyriacus — St Lawrence*
10. *St Euphemia — St Buchardus; St Martha — St Aristarchus; St Salome — St Patricia*
12. *St Anselm — St Wenceslaus; St Nemesius — St Agathion; St Huldrucus — St Januarius*
13. *St Barnabas — St Epimachus; St Titus — St Dionysius; St Crispus — St Cleophas*
14. *St Christina — St Helena; St Catherine — St Brigidia; St Clare — St Ursula*

15-19, JOHN HARDMAN & CO, 1857-60

15. *Tracery: Angels. St Bartholomew — St James Minor; St Philip — St Andrew; St Peter — St John the Evangelist*
16. *Tracery: Angels. Henry III — Henry V; St Swithun — Archbishop Waynflete; King Edward — St Edmund*
17. *Tracery: Angels. St Bernard — St Athanasius; St Gregory — St Hilary; Unidentified bishop — St Dionysius*
18. *Tracery: Angels. St Mary Magdalene — St John the Baptist; St Paul — The Virgin Mary; St Luke — St Mark*
19. *Tracery: Angels. St Martin; St Augustine*

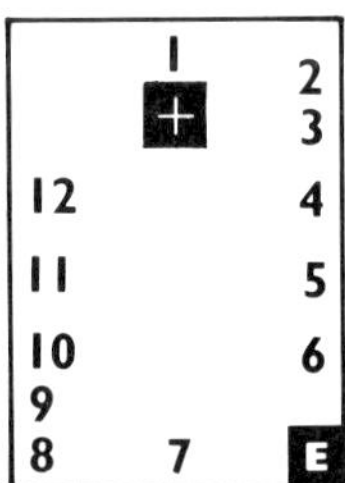

MANCHESTER COLLEGE CHAPEL

A stalwart building reflecting the serious intent of its 18th-century founders, the Unitarians. The college only transferred to Oxford from Manchester in 1880, with its buildings constructed 1891-3. The glazing of the chapel is quite outstanding, the deeply coloured foliage backgrounds to all the figures creating a leafy, almost submarine ambience.

Glass: All windows made by MORRIS & CO and designed by SIR EDWARD BURNE-JONES and WILLIAM MORRIS, 1895-9.

1. *1895. Tracery: Nativity with seraph heads. St Joseph (designed by Morris) — St Matthew; Virgin Mary — St Mark; Christ the Good Shepherd — St Paul; St Mary Magdalene (designed by MORRIS) — St Luke; St Peter — St John the Evangelist*
2. *1899. Miriam*
3. *1899. David*

4-6 were given as a memorial to a student son who died young, and contain figures of angels holding spheres illustrating the Creation story as described in Genesis.

4. *1895. The 1st Day of Creation; The 2nd Day of Creation*
5. *1895. The 3rd Day of Creation; The 4th Day of Creation*
6. *1895. The 5th Day of Creation; The 6th Day of Creation*
7. *1896. Tracery: Roundel depicting 'Teaching the Ignorant'; Minstrel Angels and seraph heads. Angel with Lute — Angels appearing to Shepherds; Truth — The Nativity; Liberty — Christ in the Carpenter's shop; Religion — Christ blessing Children; Angel with Lute — St Mary Magdalene washing Christ's feet*
8. *1896. Justice; Humility*
9. *1896. Generosity; Courage*
10. *1896. Charity (the Good Samaritan); Mercy (Dorcas)*
11. *1896. Prayer; Inspiration*
12. *1897. Faith; Prophecy*

MERTON COLLEGE CHAPEL

Merton can lay claim to be one of the earliest of Oxford colleges, and certainly has the oldest surviving buildings. It is approached through one of the city's most charming streets, which retains its old cobbles. In Mob Quad, Merton can boast the first fully evolved Oxford quadrangle. The college was founded in 1262.

Glass: The chapel contains glass of three distinct periods — the original choir glazing of the late 13th century (tracery of window 1, windows 2-8 and 18-24), late 14th-century glass made for the transepts (main lights of window 1) and the later transept glazing of the early 15th century (tracery of window 13). Windows 9-12 and 14-17, plain.

1. *This window contains glass from all periods. The tracery lights are part of the late 13th-century glazing programme, while the large scale figures (sadly cut down) date from the late 14th century and are probably by the workshop of Thomas Glasier, better known for his work at New College. They were made for the transept. The smaller figure panels are from the early 15th-century transept glazing. Tracery: At the centre of the rose motif are the arms of England (for Edward I), England with a label of 5 points (for Edward, Prince of Wales) and the great magnate family of Clare. In the outer quatrefoils are figures of the Archangel Gabriel and the Virgin Mary, the former holding the Annunciation message 'Ave Maria'. Main lights: Two seraphim standing on wheels (15th century); Crucifixion attended by the Virgin and St John (15th century); A saintly Benedictine Abbess (late 14th century); The Virgin and Child (late 14th century); A saintly Benedictine Abbess (late 14th Century); St John the Evangelist holding a chalice with serpent (late 14th century); Seraphim and Virgin Annunciate with inserted head (15th century). In a single row above, and two rows below the figures panels, is a series of ex situ 15th- and early 16th-century shields.*

2-8 and 18-24: These windows of the choir were the gift of Henry de Mamesfield, Fellow of Merton College, 1288-96, and Chancellor of the University, 1309-12; he died in 1328. He appears in 12 of the 14 windows. In each 3-light window, the figure of an apostle (not all of them identifiable) in the centre light is flanked by a figure of the donor in each of the outer lights. Only the two easternmost windows of the south wall digress from this pattern. All the donor figures either carry scrolls or kneel above strips bearing the inscription *'Henricus de Mamesfeld me fecit'* (Henry de Mamesfeld made me). The choir windows were heavily but sensitively restored by Samuel Caldwell in 1931.

2. *An Archbishop, St Paul and St Nicholas*
3. *St Lawrence, probably St Jude and St Stephen*
4. *St Thomas with donor figures.*
5. *Apostle with scroll with donor figures.*
6. *St James Major with donor figures.*
7. *Apostle with palm with donor figures.*
8. *Probably St Matthew with donor figures.*

13. *The remaining early 15th-century transept glazing is now concentrated in the tracery of the west window of the crossing and cannot easily be studied without binoculars. Some of the figures are composite but amongst them are figures of St Christopher carrying the Christ Child, St John the Baptist, St Philip, St Bartholomew, St Simon, St Matthew, St Ethelbert, St George, St Paul, St Peter, St Andrew, St James Major, St Thomas, St James Minor, St Thomas of Hereford, and the Archangel Gabriel and Virgin Mary from the Annunciation and the Virgin and Christ enthroned from the Coronation of the Virgin. The heads of the main lights contain fragments of 15th-century canopies, although these are partially obscured by the organ.*

18. *Apostle with donor figures.*
19. *Apostle with palm with donor figures.*
20. *St Bartholomew with donor figures.*
21. *Apostle with donor figures.*
22. *Apostle with donor figures.*
23. *St Andrew with donor figures.*
24. *St Peter with donor figures.*

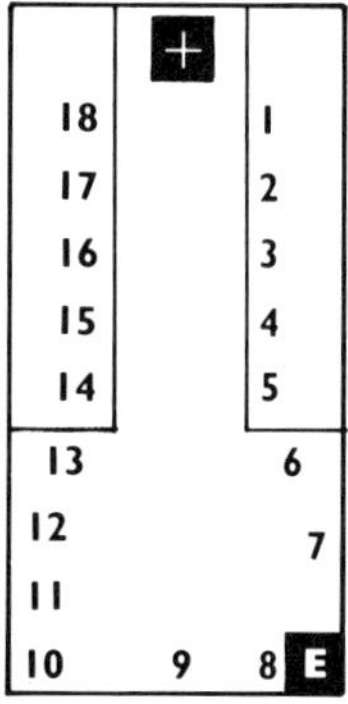

NEW COLLEGE CHAPEL

The college was founded by William of Wykeham, Bishop of Winchester, whose figure — together with that of the Virgin Mary to whom he was devoted — stands over the medieval gate; the college was built 1380-6. With its beautiful cloisters, lovely gardens and superb view of the medieval city walls, which enclose it on two sides, New College is one of Oxford's most attractive colleges for visitor and scholar alike.

Glass: By the workshop of THOMAS GLASIER of Oxford, *c.*1380-6, WILLIAM PRICE, 1735-40; WILLIAM PECKITT, 1765 and 1774, the latter after designs by BIAGIO REBECCA; THOMAS JERVAIS after designs by SIR JOSHUA REYNOLDS, 1775-85; WILLIAM RAPHAEL EGINTON, 1820-1.

1-5: The tracery lights contain representations of the Nine Orders of Angels, 1380-6. The figures below, many of them unidentifiable, are by WILLIAM PRICE The Younger, 1735-40.

1. *Tracery: Cherubim. Bishop — Male saint; Bishop — Bishop; Bishop — Pope; Archbishop — Bishop*
2. *Tracery: Dominations. Archbishop — Archbishop; Bishop — Bishop; Male saint — Bishop — Bishop; St Lawrence — Cardinal*
3. *Tracery: Seraphim. Male saint — Female saint; Archbishop — Royal figure; Bishop — Female saint; Bishop — St Catherine*
4. *Tracery: Thrones. Pope — Female saint; St John the Evangelist — Female saint; St Paul — St Agnes; Bishop — St Cecilia*
5. *Tracery: Principalities. Bishop — Female saint; Figure with sceptre — St Helen; Figure with sceptre — Female saint; Pope — Female saint. Inscribed 'W. Price has Fenestras reparavit Ao Dni 1740'.*

6-8 and 10-13, by THOMAS GLASIER of Oxford, *c.*1380-6. The building accounts for the foundation period do not survive, but it is likely that the chapel and its glazing were complete when the college took possession of its buildings on 14 April 1386. Minor work continued into the early years of the 15th century.

The surviving medieval glass comes from both the antechapel and choir and, although all the major figures are now confined to the antechapel, some impression of Wykeham's original plan can be formed. The physical division of the building into antechapel and choir was mirrored by the arrangement of the subjects in the windows. Upon entering the antechapel, the visitor encountered first the representatives of the Old Law. In the upper lights stood a series of prophets carrying Messianic texts. Below stood a series of Old Testament figures, beginning with Adam and Eve (who survive in window 10).

Turning towards the entrance to the choir, windows 6 and 13 contained four depictions of the Crucifixion, with figures of the Apostles above. Altars placed below the windows emphasized the sacrificial aspect of Christ's suffering. In the choir beyond the windows contained 80 figures of saints representing the New Law made possible through Christ's sacrifice. Some of these survive in the antechapel.

The tracery lights in both antechapel and choir preserve figures representing the nine angelic hierarchies, while the Wise Virgins were probably above the female saints in the choir windows.

The principal window in the chapel is at the west end and its subject united the two themes of the glazing scheme. The window contained the Tree of Jesse, with Doom above. The Tree of Jesse, depicting the genealogy of Christ, was dominated by the crucified Christ but inhabited by Old Testament prophets and Christ's ancestors. The Virgin Mary was also given a prominent position, thus giving honour to a figure for whom Wykeham had a particular devotion. The original glass was removed in the 18th century.

Across the base of the antechapel windows are the remains of inscriptions requesting prayers for Archbishop William of Wykeham *'Fundatore istius collegii'*.

6. *Tracery: Angels, Cherubim, Grotesques and the Virgin and Christ in Majesty. St Philip — Virgin Mary from a Crucifixion; St Bartholomew — Female saint; St Matthew — St John the Evangelist from a Crucifixion; St Simon — Virgin Mary from a Crucifixion; St Matthias — Female saint; St Jude — St John the Evangelist from a Crucifixion*
7. *Tracery: Grotesques and Cherubim. A bishop saint — St Athanasius; A pope — St Bernard; St Alphege — A bishop saint; A bishop saint — A bishop saint*
8. *Tracery: Grotesques and Seraphim. St Mary of Egypt — St Martha; probably Prophet Baruch — Female saint (wrongly labelled Anselm); Prophet Jonah — Crowned female saint; St Mary — Female saint (wrongly labelled Cuthbert)*
9. *Painted by THOMAS JERVAIS, after designs by SIR JOSHUA REYNOLDS, 1778-85. The Nativity (Reynolds and Jervais appear as two of the shepherds); The Virtues: Temperance, Fortitude, Faith, Charity, Hope, Justice, Prudence (Mrs Sheridan and other society beauties are said to have posed for these figures). The remains of the original 14th-century window can still be seen in the south choir aisle of York Minster.*
10. *Tracery: Grotesques and Thrones. Prophet Jeremiah — Adam with spade; Prophet Isaiah — Eve with distaff and spindle; Unnamed prophet — Seth; Prophet Hosea — Enoch*
11. *Tracery: Grotesques and Principalities. Prophet Amos — Patriarch Methusaleh; Prophet Jael — Patriarch Noah; Prophet Micah — Patriarch Abraham; Prophet Zephaniah — Patriarch Isaac*
12. *Tracery: Grotesques and Dominations. Prophet Daniel — Patriarch Jacob — Prophet Ezekiel — Judas Maccabeus; Prophet Obadiah — Patriarch Moses; Prophet Habakkuk — Nahum*
13. *Tracery apex: William Wykeham kneeling at the feet of the Virgin Mary. St Peter — Female saint; St Andrew — Female saint with part of Christ crucified; St James Major — St John the Evangelist from a Crucifixion; St John the Evangelist — Virgin Mary from a Crucifixion; St Thomas — probably a Deacon saint and part of a Crucifixion; St James Minor — St John the Evangelist from a Crucifixion*

14-18: The tracery lights contain representations of the Nine Orders of Angels and the Wise Virgins, *c.*1380-6. The figures below were painted by WILLIAM PECKITT of York, with the exception of St Paul and St Barnabas in 18, which were supplied by WILLIAM RAPHAEL EGINTON in 1820-1. Windows 17 and the rest of 18 were painted by PECKITT in 1765. Windows 14 to 16 were completed by him in 1774 after designs by BIAGIO REBECCA.

14. *Tracery: Powers. Baruch — Adam (1774); Hosea — Eve; Daniel — Seth; Ezekiel — Enoch*
15. *Tracery: Virtues. Joel — Methusaleh; Amos — Noah; Obadiah — Abraham; Jonah — Isaac*
16. *Tracery: Archangels. Micah — Jacob; Nahum — Judah; Habakkuk — Moses; Zephaniah — Aaron*
17. *Tracery: Angels. St James Minor — St John the Evangelist; St Thomas — Christ; St Simon — Virgin Mary; St Matthew — St Peter*
18. *Tracery: Six Wise Virgins. St Philip — St Paul; St James Major — St Barnabas; St Andrew — St Jude; St Bartholomew — St Matthias. Inscribed '[1]765 W Pec[kitt] pin[xit]'.*

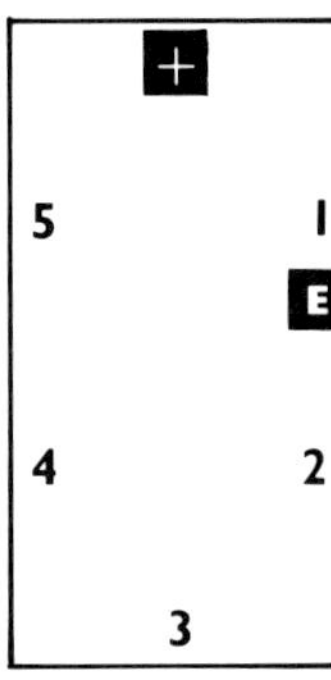

NUFFIELD COLLEGE CHAPEL

Founded in 1937 and built 1949-60 to designs by Harrison, Barnes & Hubbard. The architecture, in a modern way, reaffirms the medieval collegiate ideal; spacious quadrangles, ringed by low roofed mellow ranges, create a restful atmosphere. The chapel is in the roof and the climb up several flights of stairs enhances its sense of solitude and quiet. It is a plain room, even austere, in which the richness of the windows, set deep into the walls, excites the senses.

Glass: Designed by JOHN PIPER, made by PATRICK REYNTIENS, 1965-6. Scheme of four abstract windows and one opposite the altar, incorporating symbols of the Passion.

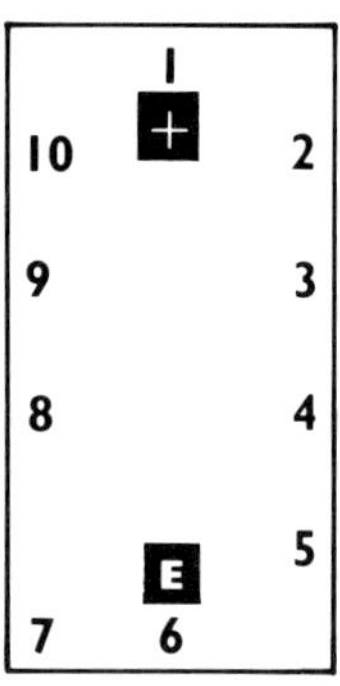

ORIEL COLLEGE CHAPEL

This college derives its name from that of a medieval house, La Oriole, acquired by the college in the 14th century. Although Oriel is a medieval foundation, what survives is mainly of the 17th century. The front quadrangle is dominated by the magnificent gabled staircase decorated with statues of Edward II and Charles I. The chapel, consecrated in 1642, stands to the right of this and incorporates an oriel window over its door.

Glass: Window 7, late 15th/early 16th century. Window 2, CLAYTON & BELL, *c.*1870. Window 5, WILLIAM PECKITT, 1767. Windows 1, 3, 4 and 8-10, designed by HARRY ELLIS WOOLDRIDGE, made by JAMES POWELL & SONS, 1885. Window 6 (oriel over door), plain.

1. *JAMES POWELL & SONS, 1885. Tracery: Annunciation after a 15th-century Italian painting. The adoration of the Magi and Shepherds.*
2. *CLAYTON & BELL, c.1870. Tracery: Angel with shield. St Longinus; St George; St Alban*
3. *JAMES POWELL & SONS, 1885. Tracery: Annunciation. St John the Evangelist; St Peter; St John the Baptist*
4. *JAMES POWELL & SONS, 1885. Tracery: Annunciation. Elisha; Moses; Abraham*
5. *WILLIAM PECKITT, 1767. The Presentation of Christ in the Temple (formerly the east window until the 1880s).*
7. *Late 15th/early 16th-century figure of St Margaret: She is crowned and carries a cross-staff. The dragon can be seen at the bottom left-hand side of the panel.*
8. *JAMES POWELL & SONS, 1885. Tracery: The Annunciation. Bewigged 17th/18th-century Lord Chancellor; An Elizabethan figure; A 17th-century Bishop*
9. *JAMES POWELL & SONS, 1885. Tracery: The Annunciation. Elizabethan scholar; Elizabethan scholar; Elizabethan scholar*
10. *JAMES POWELL & SONS, 1885. Tracery: Annunciation. Adam de Brome; King Edward III; King Edward II*

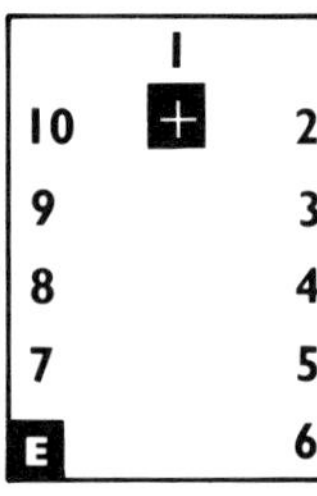

PEMBROKE COLLEGE CHAPEL

Founded in 1624, with a chapel consecrated in 1732 and now decorated sumptuously with windows by CHARLES EAMER KEMPE, an old student of the college. The glass is part of a rich scheme that covers the walls and ceiling of the chapel.

Glass: All windows by CHARLES EAMER KEMPE, 1884-*c.*1900. All windows have elaborate borders in Renaissance style, with putti, cartouches, etc.

1. *1884. The Nativity*
2. *1884/5. The Adoration of the Shepherds*
3. *1880s. The Adoration of the Magi*
4. *1892. King James I, the Earl of Pembroke, Tesdale and Wightwick (the 'Founders Window').*
5. *c.1900. The Crucifixion with attendant figures.*
6. *c.1890. Lunette window with portrait medallion.*
7. *1892. King Charles I, with attendant figures of 'Benefaction' and 'Abnegation'.*
8. *1880s. St Cyril of Alexandria and St Jerome, with 'Truth' and 'Wisdom'.*
9. *1880s. St Bernard and St Anselm, with 'Contemplation' and 'Theology'.*
10. *1884. The Annunciation*

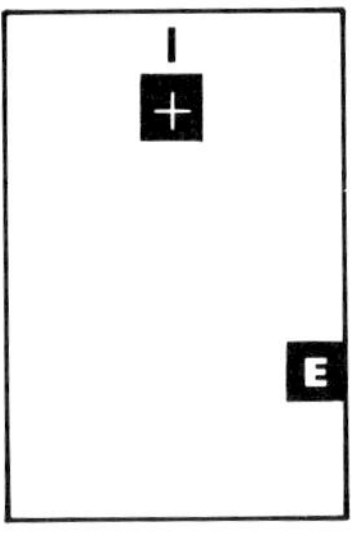

PUSEY HOUSE CHAPEL

Pusey House was founded in 1884 as a theological centre and memorial to Edward Bouverie Pusey, one of the leaders of the Oxford Movement. It was designed in the Gothic style, the architectural favourite of the Oxford Movement, by Temple Moore and built 1911-14 with additions in 1921-6. The chapel is reached via a winding cloister. It is a beautifully spacious structure, long and narrow, lit by enormous windows. The only window with stained glass is by another great (albeit late) Gothic Revivalist, J NINIAN COMPER.

1. *J NINIAN COMPER, c.1913. Tracery: Angels. Christ in Majesty with the Virgin and Child beneath, surrounded by saints and prophets in the manner of a Jesse Tree.*

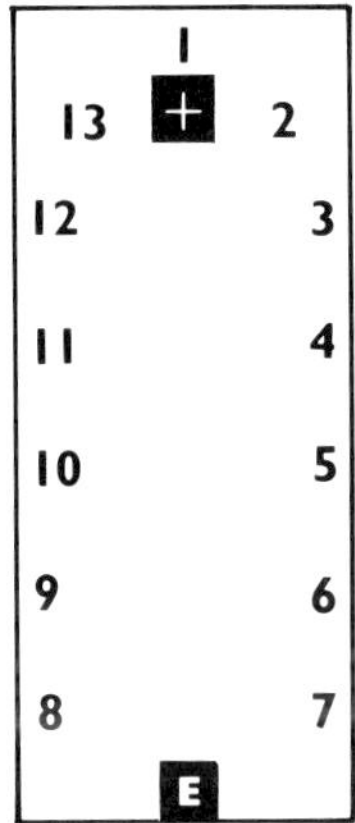

THE QUEEN'S COLLEGE CHAPEL

Although the college was founded in the 14th century, the disintegration of the medieval fabric led to substantial reconstruction between 1674 and 1760, creating Oxford's only major example of English Baroque. The front quadrangle, with its juxtaposition of hall and chapel, is one of the most impressive of Oxford façades.

Glass: All from the medieval chapel, with the exception of the east window (1), by JOSHUA PRICE, who also probably painted 7 and 8. Price set the old glass in the new chapel *c.*1717, adding winged angels' heads (1-3, 12 and 13), scenes in the lunettes (2, 3, 12 and 13), as well as many other small areas. The reset glass was 16th century (6 and 9) or by ABRAHAM VAN LINGE (2-5, 10-13), 1635, who was responsible for the Apostles (1, 2, 4-6, 9-11, 13) and winged angels' heads (4-6, 9-11) in the lunettes. Later work of the 18th and 19th centuries is in window 6.

1. *St Peter. A view of a city. St Paul. The Holy Family with angels*
2. *St Luke. The Last Supper. St John the Evangelist. The Ascension*
3. *The Flight into Egypt. The Agony in the Garden. The Resurrection*
4. *St Matthias. St Simon. The Adoration of the Shepherds*
5. *St Bartholomew. St Philip. The Pentecost*
6. *Head of the window: St Andrew — An unidentified saint (18th century). Below, three figures (each dated 1518) stand under canopies against damask hangings. Three armorials are placed at their feet — only that on the extreme R is original (arms of England set against a wreath and surmounted by a crown). The settings are post-medieval. Bishop Saint; St Clement with anchor (head, post-medieval); St Peter holding keys. Dated 1518 at base.*
7. *St Margaret — St John of Beverley; St Christopher — St Robert; St Edward the Confessor — St Anne teaching the Virgin to read*
8. *The Annunciation with the Crucifix on the Lily; St Aldhelm; St Osmund; St Lawrence*
9. *Head of the window: St James Minor — St John the Evangelist (18th century). Below, three figures (dated 1518). Settings as for window 6. St James Major dressed as a pilgrim, mitre added; Archbishop saint; Composite figure with mitre and staff*
10. *St Jude. St Thomas. The Annunciation; The Visitation*
11. *St James. St Matthew. The Last Supper; The Crucifixion*
12. *The Adoration of the Shepherds and the Magi. The Last Judgement*
13. *St Matthew. The Baptism of Christ. St Mark. The Last Judgement. Inscribed 'ABR:VAN:LINGE FECIT (6–), Refecit qe JOSa PRICE 17(–)'.*

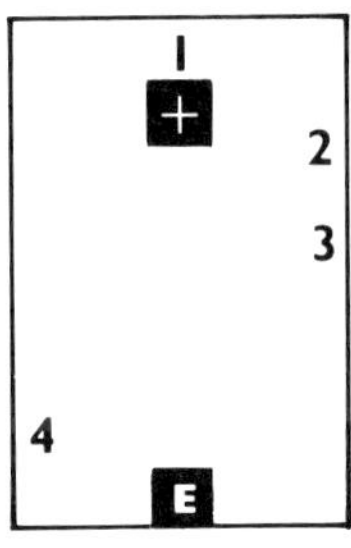

ST EDMUND HALL CHAPEL

One of Oxford's most charming colleges, named after Oxford's first canonized don, St Edmund of Abingdon, whose image can be seen in the church of St Michael at the North Gate. Until 1957, when it was made a college, St Edmund Hall was one of the last surviving medieval student halls. It offers the rare opportunity to see a working cartoon alongside a completed widow.

Glass: Window 1, MORRIS, MARSHALL, FAULKNER & CO, 1865. Windows 2-4, CLAYTON & BELL, 1865.

1. *MORRIS, MARSHALL, FAULKNER & CO, designed by EDWARD BURNE-JONES, WILLIAM MORRIS and PHILIP WEBB, 1865. Tracery: Adoration of the Lamb; Singing Angels; Minstrel Angels (BURNE-JONES). The Baptism of Christ (sketch in antechapel) — The Nativity (BURNE-JONES); The Crucifixion — The Last Supper (BURNE-JONES); The Disciples at the empty tomb (cartoon in antechapel) — The three Marys at the empty tomb (MORRIS). Pattern work in the left and right lights by PHILIP WEBB.*
2. *CLAYTON & BELL, 1865. Angel — St Peter; Angel — St Paul*
3. *CLAYTON & BELL, 1865. Angel — St Nicholas; Angel — St Edmund*
4. *CLAYTON & BELL, 1865. Angel — Virgin Mary; Angel — St John the Evangelist*

ST JOHN'S COLLEGE CHAPEL

The college was founded as St Bernard's College, a monastic (Cistercian) foundation, by Archbishop Chichele (who also founded All Souls) in 1437. It was consequently dissolved during the Reformation, and was refounded under its present name in 1555. The chapel was consecrated only a few years before the dissolution of the college but its present interior, although Gothic in style, is entirely Victorian, having been refurbished by Edward Blore in 1843. It is decorated by a splendid hammer-beam timber roof sporting carved angels and delicately patterned tracery.

Glass: Windows 2, 3, and 7, CLAYTON & BELL, 1871. Window 1, C E KEMPE, 1892. Window 4, ERVIN BOSSANYI, 1944. Window 8, UNKNOWN MAKER, *c.*1930. Windows 5 and 6, plain.

1. *CHARLES EAMER KEMPE, 1892. Tracery: Angels with shields. St John the Baptist — Sir Thomas White (16th-century founder of St John's); The Virgin Mary — The Visitation; The Crucifixion — The Adoration of the Christ Child; St John the Evangelist — The Annunciation; St Bernard — Archbishop Chichele*
2. *CLAYTON & BELL, 1871. Tracery: Angels. St Andrew — Calling of Andrew and Peter; St Peter — Christ's charge to Peter; St James Major — The Transfiguration*
3. *CLAYTON & BELL, 1871. Tracery: Angels. St Joseph of Arimathaea — The Entombment; St Paul — The Conversion of Paul; St Augustine of Canterbury — Augustine with King Ethelbert and Queen Bertha of Kent*
4. *ERVIN BOSSANYI, 1944. St Francis of Assisi freeing caged birds; St Francis healing leper (versions of windows made for the Zouche Chapel in York Minster; these panels were given by the artist's son in 1977)*
7. *CLAYTON & BELL, 1870. Tracery: Angels. Samuel — Samuel and David; David and Goliath; Elijah — Elijah and Elisha*
8. *UNKNOWN MAKER, c.*1930, Heraldry of William Laud, Richard Bayle and William Juxon.

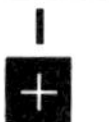

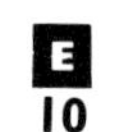

ST PETER'S COLLEGE CHAPEL

St Peter's was founded in 1928, but only achieved full college status in 1961. The chapel is the church of St Peter-le-Bailey, designed by Basil Champneys in 1874. The interior is considerably enlivened by the dramatic window over the altar, by JOHN HAYWARD, which lends vibrancy to the dim choir.

Glass: Windows 1 (tracery only) and 10, JAMES POWELL & SONS, 1880s. Window 1, main lights, JOHN HAYWARD, 1964. All other windows, plain.

1. *JOHN HAYWARD, 1964. Scenes from the Life of St Peter. (Tracery: remains of the former east window, now installed in window 10; symbols of the Evangelists, made by JAMES POWELL & SONS and designed by HENRY HOLIDAY, 1880s.)*
10. *JAMES POWELL & SONS, designed by HENRY HOLIDAY, 1880s (formerly in the east window). Tracery: Plain glazing. St Matthew — St James; St Mark — St Andrew; Christ — St Peter; St Luke — St Philip; St John — St Paul*

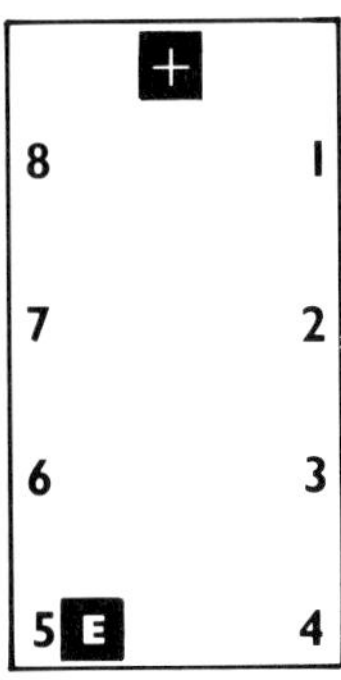

TRINITY COLLEGE CHAPEL

Trinity College was founded in 1555 but is now Oxford's most magnificent architectural manifestation of the 17th century. The chapel, entered via Durham Quad, is filled with sumptuous carved decoration, fine plasterwork and painting, creating one of the finest 17th-century interiors in the city. The appearance of so many northern saints in the windows is a reminder of the college's monastic origins, founded as Durham College in the 13th century by the Benedictines of Durham Cathedral Priory.

Glass: All windows made by JAMES POWELL & SONS, 1885 (possibly designed by H E WOOLDRIDGE with T G JACKSON). Window 5, plain.

1. *The Virgin Mary — The Annunciation*
2. *St Cuthbert*
3. *St Benedict — The Nativity*
4. *The Venerable Bede — The Adoration of the Magi*
6. *St Leonard — The three Marys at the empty tomb*
7. *St Oswald*
8. *St Catherine — The Deposition*

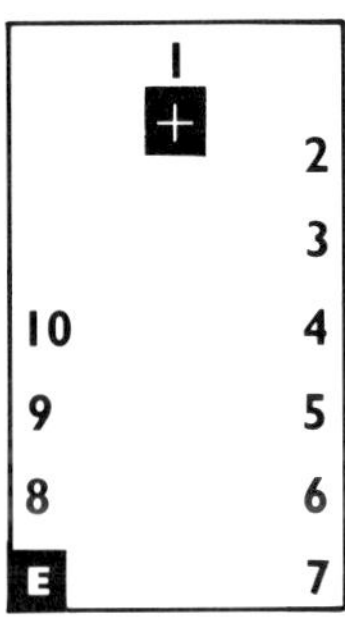

UNIVERSITY COLLEGE CHAPEL

Although University College (1249) can claim to be one of the oldest colleges in Oxford, it is structurally of the 17th and 18th centuries. The façade, with its twenty-three bays, is one of the most imposing features of the High Street. The chapel, refurbished with Gothic detail in 1862, retains one of the best preserved 17th-century glazing schemes in the city, rich in colour and full of fascinating detail.

Glass: Windows 3-10, ABRAHAM VAN LINGE, 1641. Windows 1 and 2 (MICHAEL & ARTHUR O'CONNOR, CLAYTON & BELL), 19th century.

1. *MICHAEL AND ARTHUR O'CONNOR, 1864. Tracery: Christ in Majesty with Angels. Christ before Pilate; Christ carrying the Cross; The Crucifixion with the Virgin, St John and St Mary Magdalene; The Entombment; The Resurrection*
2. *CLAYTON & BELL, 1866. Tracery: Angel with scroll. The Adoration of the Magi.*

3-10, ABRAHAM VAN LINGE, 1641. Traceries: Figures of Angels holding shields.

3. *The Temptation and Expulsion of Adam and Eve from Eden. Inscribed 'ABRAHAM VAN LINGE FECIT ANNO 1641'.*
4. *Abraham and the Angels; Adam and Eve lamenting the Fall. Inscribed as 3 above.*
5. *The Sacrifice of Isaac.*
6. *Christ in the house of Martha and Mary. Inscribed as 3 above.*
7. *Christ driving out the money-changers.*
8. *Jacob's Vision. Inscribed as 3 above.*
9. *The Translation of Elijah with Elisha catching his cloak. Inscribed as 3 above.*
10. *Jonah and the Whale. Inscribed as 3 above.*

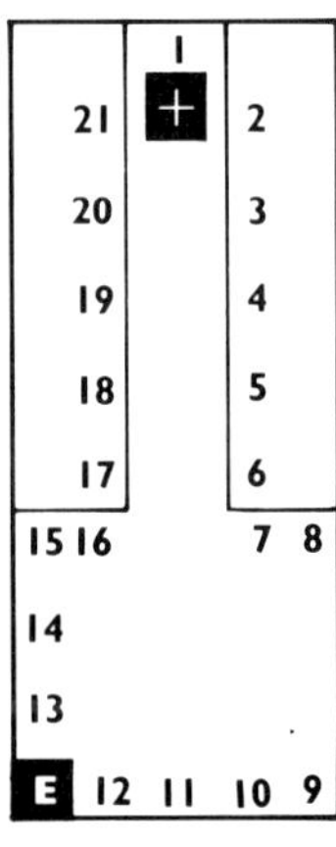

WADHAM COLLEGE CHAPEL

The great wealth of its founders, Nicholas and Dorothy Wadham, enabled Wadham College to be built in a remarkably short period — 1610-13. This very fine example of Jacobean architecture, tasteful and modest, has remained almost unchanged ever since. In scale and detail it is one of Oxford's most well-proportioned colleges. The chapel, entered by a barrel-vaulted passage, contains delicately carved stalls, a beautiful screen and some of Oxford's finest 17th-century stained glass by otherwise little-known artists.

Glass: Windows 2 and 21, early 16th century (Netherlandish). Windows 1-6 and 17-21 (BERNARD VAN LINGE, LEWIS DOLPHIN & ROBERT RUDLAND), 17th century. Windows 9-14, BETTON & EVANS. 1838. Windows 7, 8, 15 and 16, UNKNOWN MAKER, *c.*1850s.

1. *BERNARD VAN LINGE, 1622. Scenes from the Old Testament in the tracery and from the Passion in the main lights. Tracery: Translation of Elijah; Sacrifice of Isaac; The Brazen Serpent; Jonah and the Whale; The Flagellation — The Entry into Jerusalem; The Bearing of the Cross — The Agony in the Garden; The Crucifixion — The Betrayal; The Resurrection — Christ before Caiaphas; The Ascension — Pilate offers the crowd Christ or Barabbas. Inscribed 'BERNARD VAN LINGE 1622'.*

2-6, with the exception of the Netherlandish panels in 2, the figures of Christ and the Apostles with St Stephen and St Paul are probably by LEWIS DOLPHIN, 1616. Each Apostle is labelled and has a sentence of the Creed.

2. *16th-century Pentecost, heavily restored, in upper lights. Of Netherlandish origin, given to the college in 1836. Lower lights: Christ; St Peter; St Andrew (17th century)*
3. *St John; St Bartholomew; St Philip*
4. *St James Major; St Thomas; St Matthew*
5. *St James Minor; St Simon; St Jude*
6. *St Matthias (1616); St Paul; St Stephen (1616)*

7 & 8, UNKNOWN MAKER, c.1850s. Heraldic

9. *BETTON & EVANS, 1838. Abraham; Moses; Aaron*
10. *BETTON & EVANS, 1838. Gideon; Joshua; Elijah*

11 & 12 are obscured by the organ.

11. *BETTON & EVANS, 1838. Saul; David; Solomon*
12. *BETTON & EVANS, 1838. Three prophets*

13 & 14, probably by BETTON & EVANS, 1840s. Heraldic

15 & 16, UNKNOWN MAKER (as for 7 & 8). Heraldic

17 & 21: With exception of the Netherlandish panels in 21, the figures of prophets in 19 and Ezekiel in 20 are perhaps by ROBERT RUDLAND OF OXFORD, *c.*1614. The prophets in 17, 18, 20 (other than Ezekiel) and 21 are probably by BERNARD VAN LINGE, *c.*1622.

17. *Malachi (16–); Zachariah; Haggai*
18. *Habakkuk; Micah; Jonah*
19. *Obadiah; Amos; Joel*
20. *Hosea; Daniel; Ezekiel*
21. *16th-century Adoration of the Christ Child, with attendant donors, heavily restored, in upper lights. Set in an architectural setting with landscape background. Of Netherlandish origin. Given to the college in 1836. Lower lights: Jeremiah; Isaiah; David (17th century)*

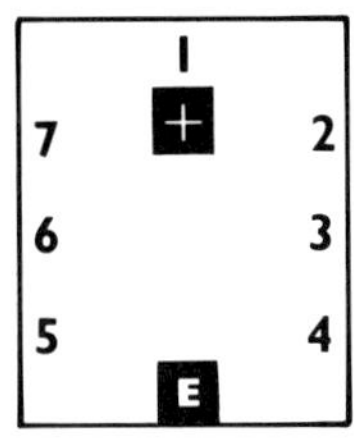

WORCESTER COLLEGE CHAPEL

The chapel was completed in 1791, then redecorated in 1864 by William Burges and Henry Holiday. The windows, executed in vivid colours, are a powerful complement to the frieze of gesturing figures that encircle the walls.

Glass: All windows made by LAVERS & BARRAUD and designed by HENRY HOLIDAY, 1864-5.

1. *Crucifixion with the Virgin and St John*
2. *The Ascension*
3. *The Baptism of Christ*
4. *The Adoration of the Magi*
5. *The Annunciation*
6. *Christ before the Elders in the Temple*
7. *The three Marys at the empty tomb*

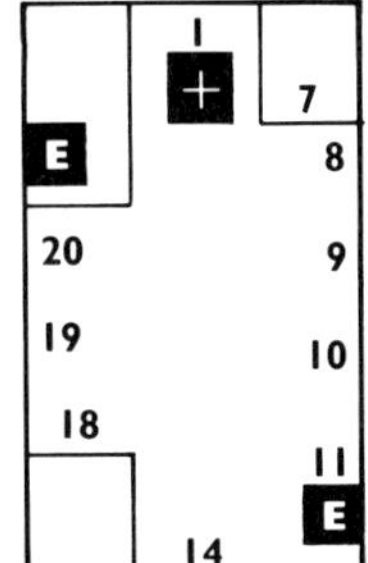

CHURCH OF ST MARY THE VIRGIN

The parish church of Oxford, spacious, airy and well-proportioned. Before the building of the Sheldonian Theatre, this was the venue for all Oxford University ceremonies. The University's first library was housed in the Congregation House. One of the church's most splendid features is its elaborate south porch of 1637, by Nicholas Stone.

Glass: Window 1, a few medieval fragments in tracery. Windows 7-11 and 14 (WILLIAM WAILES & A W N PUGIN, CLAYTON & BELL, JOHN HARDMAN & CO, C E KEMPE), 19th century. Windows 18-20, UNKNOWN MAKER, *c.*1900. Windows 2-6, 12-13, 15-17 and 21-26, plain.

1. *MEDIEVAL FRAGMENTS. A few indistinct fragments at the top of the tracery. Part of a face. Mostly 15th century.*
7. *WILLIAM WAILES, designed by AUGUSTUS WELBY NORTHMORE PUGIN, 1843. Tracery: Angels. Scenes from the Life of St Thomas: Kneeling donors, those commemorated and Annunciation beneath main subject.*
8. *CLAYTON & BELL, 1873. Tracery: Angels with musical instruments. David; Miriam; The Virgin Mary; Simeon*
9. *JOHN HARDMAN & CO, designed by AUGUSTUS WELBY NORTHMORE PUGIN, 1854. Tracery: Angels. Four incidents in Christ's Ministry involving women. Female figure commemorated depicted in lower right-hand corner of window.*
10. *JOHN HARDMAN & CO, designed by JOHN HARDMAN POWELL, c.1865. Tracery: Angels; The Tree of Jesse*
11. *CLAYTON & BELL, 1870s. Tracery: Angels. The Four Evangelists, with four doctors of the Church beneath*
14. *CHARLES EAMER KEMPE, 1891. Tracery: Angels with shields. Tree of Jesse*

18, 19 and 20, Shields set in rectangular quarries. Maker/designer unknown, probably 1900.

BIBLIOGRAPHY

Books for further reading

General

E S Greening Lambourn, *The Armorial Glass of the Oxford Diocese, 1250-1850* (1949).

N Pevsner and J Sherwood, *The Buildings of England: Oxfordshire* (1974).

Royal Commission on Historical Monuments, England, *An Inventory of the Historical Monuments in the City of Oxford* (1939).

Paul San Casciani, *The Stained Glass of Oxford.*

The Middle Ages

H W Garrod, *Ancient Painted Glass in Merton College, Oxford* (1931).

C H Grinling, 'Ancient Stained Glass in Oxford', in *Oxford Architectural and Historical Society* (1883).

F E Hutchinson, *Medieval Glass at All Souls College* (1949).

Peter A Newton, 'Stained Glass at Oxford', in N Pevsner and J Sherwood, *The Buildings of England: Oxfordshire* (1974).

Peter A Newton, *Corpus Vitrearum Medii Aevi: The County of Oxford* (1979).

Christopher Woodforde, *The Stained Glass of New College, Oxford* (1951).

The 17th and 18th Centuries

Michael Archer, 'English Painted Glass in the 17th Century: The Early Work of Abraham van Linge', in *Apollo* (January, 1975), pp 26-31.

Michael Archer, 'Stained Glass at Erddig and the Work of William Price', in *Apollo* (October, 1985), pp 252-63.

L G Black, 'The College Chapel Windows', in *University College Record* (1977), pp 122-36.

J T Brighton, 'Henry Gyles, Virtuoso and Glass-Painter of York, 1645-1709', in *York Historian* (1984), vol. 4.

The 19th and 20th Centuries

R Dixon and S Muthesius, *Victorian Architecture* (1978).

E Liddall Armitage, *Stained Glass* (1960).

Martin Harrison, *Victorian Stained Glass* (1980).

A C Sewter, *The Stained Glass of William Morris and his Circle*, 2 vols. (1974-5).

Christopher Whall, *Stained Glass Work* (1905).

INDEX OF ARTISTS

INDEX

For pages 5 to 59.

Picture Credits

Chris Buckley: *Page 62(a);* ***Peter Cormack:*** *Pages 4(c), 30, 38, 41(a,b), 42, 44, 45, 46, 49, 50(a,b), 53, 54, 56, 58(a,b);* ***D E O'Connor:*** *Pages 14(b), 18;* ***T W French:*** *Pages 17;* ***K P Gingell:*** *Page 62(b,d);* ***Royal Commission on the Historical Monuments of England:*** *Front Cover, pages 4(a), 13, 14(a), 20, 60, 64;* ***Thomas-Photos:*** *Pages 4(b), 6, 9, 10, 22, 27, 28, 33, 34, 37, 62(c), back cover.*

Front Cover: *Quatrefoil showing St Augustine of Canterbury preaching to a group of monks and laymen. 14th Century, Lucy Chapel, Christ Church Cathedral.*

Back Cover: *St Michael and his Angels fighting the Dragons. 19th century, Christ Church Cathedral.*